THE GOLDEN GARUDA

The great Jigme Phuntsok Rinpoche, France, 1993.

The Golden Garuda

The Extraordinary Life of Modern-Day
Mahasiddha Jigme Phuntsok Rinpoche

Khenpo Sodargye

TRANSLATED BY
The Wisdom and Compassion
Translation Group

SHAMBHALA

Shambhala Publications, Inc.
2129 13th Street
Boulder, Colorado 80302
www.shambhala.com

© 2025 by Khenpo Sodargye
Page 241 constitutes a continuation of the copyright page.

Cover photo: Jigme Phuntsok Rinpoche
Cover art: Courtesy of Robert Beer
Cover design: Daniel Urban-Brown

9 8 7 6 5 4 3 2 1

First Edition
Printed in the United States of America

Shambhala Publications makes every effort to print
on acid-free, recycled paper.
Shambhala Publications is distributed worldwide by
Penguin Random House, Inc., and its subsidiaries.

LIBRARY OF CONGRESS CATALOGING-IN-PUBLICATION DATA
Names: Suodaji, Kanbu, 1962– author. | Suodaji, Kanbu, 1962– Snyigs dus
bstan pa'i gsal byed gcig pu chos rje dam pa yid bzhin nor bu 'jigs med phun
tshogs 'byung gnas dpal bzang po'i rnam thar bsdus pa dad pa'i gsos sman.
Title: The golden garuda: the extraordinary life of modern-day Mahasiddha
Jigme Phuntsok Rinpoche / Khenpo Sodargye; translated by The Wisdom
and Compassion Translation Group.
Other titles: Snyigs dus bstan pa'i gsal byed gcig pu chos rje dam pa yid
bzhin nor bu 'jigs med phun tshogs 'byung gnas dpal bzang po'i rnam thar
bsdus pa dad pa'i gsos sman. English
Description: Boulder: Shambhala Publications, 2025. | Includes
bibliographical references. | Identifiers: LCCN 2024009177 | ISBN
9781645473190 (trade paperback)
Subjects: LCSH: 'Jigs-med-phun-tshogs, Mkhan-po, 1933–2004. | Rnying-
ma-pa lamas—China—Golog Zangzu Zizhizhou—Biography.
Classification: LCC BQ966.J54 S8613 2025 | DDC 294.3/923092 [B]—dc23/
eng/20240511
LC record available at https://lccn.loc.gov/2024009177

Contents

TRANSLATORS' ACKNOWLEDGMENTS

In preparing this translation, we were greatly impressed by the dedication shown to this project by Khenpo Zhicheng of Larung Gar. He answered many of our questions so that we could make the English translation as accurate as possible. Sangye Khandro of the Light of Berotsana Translation Group translated Khenpo Sodargye Rinpoche's supplication offering to the great Jigme Phuntsok Rinpoche, which you can find at the end of the book. We are deeply grateful for her masterful translation and warmhearted support.

In this biography, Khenpo Sodargye Rinpoche included the extraordinary *vajra* songs, or songs of realization, of the great Jigme Phuntsok Rinpoche, using his own Tibetan-to-Chinese translation. When we translated them from Chinese to English, the vajra songs became ordinary due to our limited capacities and lack of practical experience. We are very thankful that Orgyen Chowang Rinpoche, who was in the first small groups that were trained directly under the great Jigme Phuntsok Rinpoche back in the early 1980s, allowed us to use his extraordinary English translation of the vajra songs from Tibetan.

We would like to express our heartfelt gratitude to Adam Pearcey from Lotsawa House for granting us permission to use his translation of Jigme Phuntsok Rinpoche's prayer *The Sun of Samantabhadra's Realm: The Quintessence of Oceanic Prayers of Aspiration*.

We offer special thanks to Lea Growth-Wilson for editing the first draft of this translation and to Cecilia Luk for her tireless line editing of the first draft of the manuscript.

We extend our heartfelt appreciation to Nikko Odiseos, Tasha

Kimmet, Dianna Able, and other highly competent members of Shambhala Publications. It has been truly uplifting to work with the Shambhala team again.

We are deeply grateful for the support that Khenpo Sodargye Rinpoche has provided to us during the preparation of this translation. It is a great honor for us to have the opportunity to translate this biography. Any errors in name spellings, word choice, meaning, or understanding are entirely our own, and we ask for forgiveness from the great Jigme Phuntsok Rinpoche, Khenpo Sodargye Rinpoche, deities, dakinis, and dharmapalas for all mistakes resulting from our lack of knowledge, experience, unawareness, or otherwise.

May this biography inspire all its readers.

—The Wisdom and Compassion Translation Group
March 19, 2024

PREFACE

Homage to Manjushri!

In the boundless expanse of time and space, with their unsurpassable wisdom, unconditional compassion, and unobstructed miraculous powers, buddhas and bodhisattvas continuously come into this world in myriad forms to alleviate the suffering of countless sentient beings trapped in samsara. Their extraordinary activities are unfathomable to ordinary beings.

Among these buddhas and bodhisattvas is my peerless root lama, the Great Dharma King of Wish-Fulfilling Jewel, Jigme Phuntsok Rinpoche (1933–2004), who has taken different rebirths, life after life, in all the realms of the ten directions to benefit sentient beings and propagate the Dharma. His enlightened activities are as vast as the ocean, which can hardly be fully perceived by realized bodhisattvas, let alone by an ordinary person like me.

Setting aside the immeasurable merits that the great Jigme Phuntsok Rinpoche[1] has accumulated throughout his past lives, his extraordinary qualities and Dharma activities in this very life have profoundly inspired numerous individuals who have a karmic connection with him and guided them onto the path of liberation.

The great Jigme Phuntsok Rinpoche established deep connections with people in both the East and the West. The Larung Gar Five Sciences Buddhist Academy that he founded in the early 1980s has become one of the world's largest and most influential Tibetan Buddhist academies, where tens of thousands of Tibetan- and Chinese-speaking Dharma students benefit from a rigorous study and practice program. Compelled by his great compassion, the great Jigme Phuntsok Rinpoche also took Dharma trips to North

America, Europe, and Southeast Asia, where he conferred teachings, empowerments, and transmissions on many people, thereby forging auspicious Dharma connections with them.

Soon after my monastic ordination, I began accompanying my peerless lama on his teaching tours in both the East and the West. In recent years, I have also tried to find time to teach the Dharma overseas. From my own perspective, some Westerners I encountered during my tours are characterized by their directness and logical thinking; they are interested in philosophy and have an earnest quest for truth. These traits are aligned with the rational wisdom celebrated in Tibetan Buddhism. If these same Western practitioners also allow themselves to be guided by heart—to cultivate the emotional wisdom arising from their faith in the Three Jewels and the teacher—their practice will be transcendent. Otherwise, studying the Dharma merely mirrors engaging in worldly academic research that provides some intellectual knowledge with little transformation of the mind.

All accomplishments in Vajrayana practice hinge entirely on devotion to the teacher, or *guru* in Sanskrit and *lama* in Tibetan. The highly realized yogi Tilopa once asserted:

> To attain Buddhahood within a single lifetime, you must enter the Vajrayana path.
> To achieve realization in Vajrayana practice, you must rely upon devotion to the vajra guru.
> To cultivate guru devotion, you must believe in the guru's qualities.
> To believe in the guru's qualities, you must be acquainted with the guru's life story.

Therefore, in 2001, I wrote this biography of the great Jigme Phuntsok Rinpoche during his lifetime, and in 2014, I added the final chapter about his *parinirvana*, or passing away, to allow individuals from all walks of life—regardless of whether they have encountered or followed him—to acquaint themselves with his extraordinary qualities. I hope this biography, like a drop of water, provides readers with a glimpse into the vastness of my peerless lama's ocean of great qualities.

As said by Jamgön Mipham Rinpoche (1846–1912), the incomparable Dharma master from the Land of Snows, one should refrain from praising anyone, including one's own root lama, with empty and untruthful words. Therefore, this biography maintains an objective and truthful stance throughout. Every event herein is recounted devoid of fabrication and exaggeration and was witnessed by, or known to, numerous disciples of the great Jigme Phuntsok Rinpoche.

Throughout his life, my peerless lama placed significant emphasis on teaching and practicing the Dharma. Hence, this biography predominantly focuses on documenting his Dharma activities and spiritual journeys, giving little attention to his interactions with government officials and social elites as well as his involvement in political matters.

My peerless lama rarely disclosed or discussed his profound spiritual attainments. This book, therefore, does not delve into his secret biography, including his direct visions of deities and his uncommon spiritual accomplishments. What is briefly disclosed in this biography pertains solely to his common accomplishments, such as luminous dreams, which are nonetheless difficult to achieve by ordinary people.

This biography was originally written in Chinese with the intent to introduce my peerless lama to his Chinese followers. As a Tibetan monk, I lack proficiency in Chinese writing, so the text in the biography might lack eloquence and could potentially contain linguistic errors. The English translation of this biography, meant to acquaint Westerners with my peerless lama, has possibly inherited similar problems. Nevertheless, with sincere intentions, I herein introduce to English readers my peerless lama, the great Jigme Phuntsok Rinpoche, one of the greatest Dzogchen (Great

Perfection) masters of the twentieth century, and his vast array of Dharma activities.

May this biography bring benefit to all its readers.

—Sodargye
August 1, 2022
(the fourth day of the sixth month
of the Tibetan calendar)
Larung Gar, Sertar

THE GOLDEN GARUDA

Above: Jigme Phuntsok Rinpoche, Larung Gar Five Sciences Buddhist Academy, 1984. In this photo Rinpoche is bestowing the empowerment of *Nyingtik Yabshi* (Four Parts of Heart Essence) on the sangha.

Bottom: Jigme Phuntsok Rinpoche's seal and fingerprint.

MANIFESTATIONS THROUGHOUT MANY LIVES

In countless lifetimes, the great Jigme Phuntsok Rinpoche has manifested various forms for the sake of benefiting sentient beings. According to historical records, some of these manifestations are as follows:

When the primordial Buddha Samantabhadra, in the absolute expanse of Akanishtha, turned the Dharma Wheel of the ultimate, the luminous Great Perfection (Tib. *Dzogchen*), the great Jigme Phuntsok Rinpoche was the compiler of the teachings, named Bodhisattva Vajragarbha (Tib. Dorjé Nyingpo), meaning "vajra essence."

He was Devaputra Adhicitta, meaning "the god's son of superior mind," the holder of Dzogchen in the Heaven of the Thirty-Three.

He was the compiler of the Glorious Vajradhara's[2] tantric teachings, named Bodhisattva Jnanagarbha (Tib. Yeshe Nyingpo), meaning "wisdom essence."

In the presence of the twelve founding teachers of Dzogchen, he was the compiler of the three inner tantras,[3] named Vajragarbha.

He was the maternal aunt of Buddha Shakyamuni, named Mahapajapati Gotami.

He was the mother of the first human Dzogchen master, Garab Dorjé, named Sudharmā.

He was the chief disciple of Manjushrimitra,[4] named Drazé Yishyin Pal, meaning "the wish-fulfilling auspiciousness."

Guru Rinpoche Padmasambhava, the second Buddha who was born in the land of Oddiyana, gave the ultimate tantric teachings at the Eight Great Charnel Grounds in India, and Jigme Phuntsok

Rinpoche was Padmasambhava's Dharma successor, Shakyamitra. He was also Jinamitra—a king of Nepal—and Nanam Dorjé Dudjom⁵—one of Padmasambhava's twenty-five main disciples in Tibet.

He was Tropu Lotsāwa⁶ Jampa Pel (1172–1236), a great translator during the later, or second, propagation of Buddhism in Tibet. He was the great *vidyadhara*⁷ Gödem Ngödrup Gyaltsen (1337–1408), the great vidyadhara Lekden Dorjé (1452–1565), Ngakgi Wangpo (1580–1639), Tertön⁸ Pema Trinlé (1641–1717), and Tertön Sogyal Lerab Lingpa (1856–1926).

Furthermore, to guide beings with different levels of spiritual capacity and to propagate the teachings of various schools and lineages, the great Jigme Phuntsok Rinpoche also manifested himself in India and Tibet as holders of different schools and lineages. Tertön Pawo Chöying Dorjé (1895–1945) described Jigme Phuntsok Rinpoche's previous lives in his *terma*,⁹ or hidden treasure:

> In ancient times, he was India's Arhat Sagilha,
> Nanam Dorjé Dudjom in Padmasambhava's presence,
> Sakya Throne Holder Kunga Gyaltsen,
> Geluk honorable master Khedrup Gelek Pelzang,
> And Kunzang Chödrak from Minyak.

Jigme Phuntsok Rinpoche was the arhat Sagilha from India who authored the *Vinaya*¹⁰ *Flower Garland*, and under the guidance of Padmasambhava, he was the vidyadhara Nanam Dorjé Dudjom. He was the throne holder of the Sakya lineage, Sakya Pandita Kunga Gyaltsen (1182–1251), who was an emanation of Bodhisattva Manjushri. He was Khedrup Gelek Pelzang (1385–1438), one of the two chief disciples of Lama Tsongkhapa (1357–1419), the founder of the Geluk school of Tibetan Buddhism. Later, he was Kunzang Chödrak¹¹ (1823–1905) from Minyak, a chief disciple of Patrul Rinpoche and the author of *The Extensive Commentary on The Way of the Bodhisattva.*

According to the terma revealed by Tertön Dribdral Rigpé Dorjé:[12]

> The honored one was once the Dharma King Drogön Chögyal Phagpa (1235–1280), the lineage holder Minling Terchen Gyurme Dorjé (1646–1714), the great learned master from Dawu[13] named Lhalung Paldor (ninth century), and Tertön Lerab Lingpa, among others.

> After five more lifetimes, Lerab Lingpa will be the commander of the Kalachakra[14] warriors, who will descend onto the human realm with his 50,000 followers to subdue proponents of non-Buddhist views. By then, whoever has been fortunate enough to build a connection with him will be reborn in the Realm of Shambhala.

Prophecies of the Incarnations

The great Jigme Phuntsok Rinpoche's existence was prophesied more than 2,500 years ago by Buddha Shakyamuni, as noted in *The Root Tantra of Manjushri*, which says:

> The eminent master whose name contains "Ah,"
> Will uphold the true teachings of the Buddha,
> And have wisdom, qualities, and respect from others.
> He is prophesied to attain the perfect enlightenment,
> And will fully realize my enlightened mind.

The "Ah" mentioned here refers to the first letter of Jigme Phuntsok Rinpoche's Sanskrit name, Ah Bhya Laksham.

Further specification of his names and incarnations was given by Padmasambhava more than 1,200 years ago about Jigme Phuntsok Rinpoche's preceding, present, and two future lives, as noted in *The Profound Mirror of Illusions*:

> My son Nanam Dorjé Dudjom,
> In Nyarong of Kham,
> On the bank of a calm river,
> In front of three majestic snowy peaks,
> Will be reborn as a tantric master in a year of the dragon,
> And become known as the notable Lerab Lingpa,
> Who will practice the supreme Vajrayana,
> And reveal numerous termas.
> If conditions naturally come together,
> He will dispel calamities arising in the turbid age,

And widely propagate the Sutrayana and Vajrayana
    teachings.
This great tertön will live on earth
Until the age of eighty-one years.

Seven of his disciples will attain Buddhahood,
One hundred and five of his followers will attain middling
    accomplishments,
And over four thousand people will establish connections
    with him.

His next incarnation will be born in Dokham[15] in a year of
    the bird.
His name will contain "Ah" and he will master the
    Tripitaka.[16]
His teachings will remain in the world for three thousand
    years.
Nine hundred of his followers will attain great
    accomplishment,
Over six thousand yogis will follow him,
And seventy thousand people will establish connections
    with him.
The great master will live to the age of eighty-six.

His next incarnation will be born in U-Tsang,
In a year of the tiger, and be given a name meaning
    "auspiciousness."
He will live in this world for thirty-three years,
And his teachings will remain for two hundred years.
Three of his disciples will attain accomplishment,
And over one thousand people will establish connections
    with him.

Three lifetimes after that,[17]
At the juncture of Kham and U-Tsang,

He will be reborn in a wealthy family in a year of the
    dragon.
He will fully possess skillful means,
And his name will be Dorjé Thomed Tsal.[18]
He will attain mastery of all termas,
And widely propagate the Dharma and benefit living
    beings.
Samaya!

Tertön Lerab Lingpa himself also clearly described the seven
signs pertaining to his immediate incarnation. As written in his
Text of Future Prophecies:

The emanation of Nanam Dorjé Dudjom,
Will be born in a bird year at the place called "the source of
    Dharma."
The name of the father will mean "lotus,"
And that of the mother will mean "turquoise lake,"
His palm will have *dakini*[19] marks.
He will teach the ocean-like Tripitaka,
And realize the primordial nature of Dharmakaya.

The details regarding the birthplace and time, parents' names,
physical characteristics, level of realization, and so on of the reincarnated child—that is, Jigme Phuntsok Rinpoche—will each be
explained in the following chapters.

TERTÖN LERAB LINGPA'S
INCREDIBLE STORIES

Jigme Phuntsok Rinpoche's immediate predecessor, the renowned Tibetan tertön Lerab Lingpa, was born amid numerous auspicious signs on an auspicious date in 1856, the year of the fire dragon according to the Tibetan calendar, in Nyarong[20] county in today's Sichuan Province. His father, Zhiwa Dargyé, was a wise and courageous man with spiritual accomplishment. His mother, Orgyen Drölma, an emanation of a wisdom dakini, was gentle and virtuous. Padmasambhava prophesied:

> The emanation of Nanam Dorjé Dudjom,
> The blessed one with wisdom and great compassion,
> Owing to his great aspirations,
> Will be born in Nyarong of Dokham in the fire dragon year.
> His father's birth year is dragon and his mother's is monkey.

And in *Lotus Instructions*, Padmasambhava gave further prophecies:

> The body manifestation of Nanam Dorjé Dudjom,
> The speech manifestation of Vajravarahi,
> The mind manifestation of Padmasambhava—
> The great compassionate one with the ultimate wisdom,
> Will be born in Dokham and named "Leling"[21]
> In the year of the fire dragon.
> Through various extraordinary actions,
> He will benefit beings and fulfill their wishes.

7

In *Future Prophecies*, Dodrupchen Jigme Trinlé Özer (1745–1821) also prophesied:

> The emanation of Nanam Dorjé Dudjom
> Will be born in Nyarong.
> Establishing a Dharma connection with him
> Is like meeting Padmasambhava in person.

There are many similar prophecies of this kind. Ever since his birth, Lerab Lingpa had been quite different from others. Once, when he was still very young, he went hunting in the woods with a group of people. Due to obscuration from transmigrating,[22] he picked up a rifle and aimed it at one of the animals in front of him. As he was about to shoot, the animals suddenly appeared to him as various deities and dakini script—the symbols or codes to unlock termas. In an instant, his innate nature was awakened, as if he had just abruptly woken up from a dream. He dropped the rifle, jumped with joy, and said repeatedly, "I get it! I get it!"

Later Lerab Lingpa studied the Dharma under the guidance of Patrul Rinpoche (1808–1887), Jigme Yönten Gönpo (1837–1898), and other great masters. Owing to his extraordinary level of wisdom, he fully mastered all the teachings he received within a short time.

Due to his aspirations in former lives to reveal termas, Lerab Lingpa started to travel across the Land of Snows, revealing profound hidden teachings that bring benefits to living beings. In Tibetan places in U-Tsang, Amdo, and Kham, he revealed many precious termas through the support of consort yoga, or *karmamudra*.[23] Padmasambhava once said:

> The boundless treasures of my termas are
> The vast, profound, and extraordinary teachings.
> My heart-son with little grasping, great wisdom, and
> superior conviction—Nanam Dorjé Dudjom

Tertön Lerab Lingpa, the great Jigme Phuntsok Rinpoche's
immediate predecessor.

Will be reborn in the future in a fire dragon year, as Lerab
Lingpa.
He will reveal my termas in Dokham and U-Tsang,
And engage in various yogic activities.
If no demonic adversities arise,
He will live on earth for over seventy years.

Lerab Lingpa's secret biography, which contains more than 360 loose-leaf pages, includes many incredible stories. Here are a few of them that may inspire you:

1. In front of Nyarong's sacred mountain Lhadrak, thousands of Buddhist devotees gathered, eager to witness the moment when Tertön Lerab Lingpa would reveal a terma. The great tertön casually extended his hand into a rock as if he were reaching into an empty space and instantly took out a forearm-length statue of Buddha Amitabha. The onlookers couldn't help but exclaim in amazement.

2. Once, when Tertön Lerab Lingpa was revealing termas in Qinghai Province, the local gods and earth spirits were somehow upset and started to create obstacles by casting heavy hail. Lerab Lingpa remained entirely unharmed. Moreover, to discipline the local gods and earth spirits, apart from revealing the intended termas, Lerab Lingpa also confiscated all their possessions. As a result, the gods and spirits who had orchestrated obstructions felt great remorse and repented before the great tertön.

3. In the year when the demonic army from the barbarian regions invaded Tibet for the ninth time and was about to destroy Buddhism, the Tibetan army was unable to resist the fierce demonic army. Tibet was in imminent danger.

Many great Tibetan masters supplicated Lerab Lingpa to subdue the demonic legions. Through his practice, Lerab Lingpa was able to find a piece of rock on which the consciousness of the demonic army's leader was residing, and he tied the rock to a tree. However, at night the attendants failed to heed Lerab Lingpa's instructions, so the rock managed to escape.

Tertön Lerab Lingpa immediately set out to search everywhere, and along the way he met seven gallant horsemen, who said, "A strange rock has leaped and hopped in that direction." Lerab Lingpa chased after it and soon caught it. He bound the rock with iron wire and thrust his *phurba*, a ritual dagger in Tibetan Buddhism, into it. At once a gush of blood spattered everywhere.

At the same time, the demonic army had surrounded the Potala Palace in Lhasa and was about to enter the Jokhang Temple, when the chief commander of the army suddenly bled from his seven orifices and dropped dead on the ground. The demonic soldiers were so horrified that they desperately withdrew from Lhasa. Thus, the Land of Snows was able to survive a catastrophe.

4. Once when Lerab Lingpa was in a state of meditative absorption, he had a direct vision of Padmasambhava as tall as a two-story building. Padmasambhava conferred on him the teaching on the three extraordinaries, then transformed into light and vanished.

5. When circumambulating the sacred mountain Tsari, Lerab Lingpa had a clear vision of Padampa Sangye (eleventh century), who transformed into the seed syllables of the five buddhas and merged into his heart. Owing to this cause and condition, he composed seven *sadhanas*[24] of practices.

6. Once on the sacred Mount Mudo, Lerab Lingpa met a majestic yogi who imparted profound teachings to him. After that, the yogi transformed into a sphere of light.

7. In Sertar, in Lerab Lingpa's pure vision there appeared over a thousand dakinis, who offered him beautiful *vajra* dances.[25] In the end, the dakinis all merged into one another, and only sixteen of them were left. Some of the sixteen dakinis were dressed in Khampa clothes, some in Amdo outfits, and others even in traditional Han Chinese garments. Two of the Chinese-dressed dakinis told him sixteen prophecies about the rise and fall of Tibetan Buddhism in the future.

8. In 1888, the year of the earth mouse, the Thirteenth Gyalwa Rinpoche Thubten Gyatso (1876–1933) invited

Lerab Lingpa to Lhasa. When they visited a sacred site under the throne of a Hayagriva[26] statue, Lerab Lingpa revealed a statue of the female deity Vajravarahi. At the Jokhang Temple, he revealed the terma *Heart Essence of the Wish-Fulfilling Jewel.* Later, Lerab Lingpa bestowed empowerments and imparted pith instructions to the Thirteenth Gyalwa Rinpoche, the Fifteenth Karmapa Khakyab Dorjé (1871–1922), the Sakya Trizin Kunga Nyingpo (1850–1899), the third Dodrupchen Jigme Tenpai Nyima (1865–1926), and other eminent masters. In particular, the Thirteenth Gyalwa Rinpoche and Jamyang Khyentse Wangpo (1820–1892) were the main holders of his teachings.

The great tertön Lerab Lingpa could reveal termas and have direct visions of deities as easily as walking on flat ground. When his Dharma activities of benefiting beings in this lifetime were about to be completed, his words and actions indicated that his "finale" was approaching. One day, Lerab Lingpa had a conversation with Jigme Tenpai Nyima. When the conversation was over and Lerab Lingpa was about to leave, he told Jigme Tenpai Nyima, "We have no chance to meet again in this life in this impure realm. I will see you again in the pure land."

Before entering parinirvana—his final passing away—Lerab Lingpa not only hinted that his next incarnation would propagate the Dharma at Nubzur Monastery in Sertar, but he also made explicit prophecies. For instance, in his later years, when Lerab Lingpa came to Nubzur Monastery and gave the empowerment of *The Wrathful Padmasambhava Practice* to the *tulku*—an incarnation of a Buddhist master—and to other sangha members at Nubzur Monastery, he said, "A few years from now, I will come and live here and give Sutrayana and Vajrayana teachings to many people. At that time, Lama Tashul will be the assistant teacher, and you'll build me a house. To make sure this future occurrence is free from any obstacles, the sangha at Nubzur Monastery should practice *The*

Most Secret Sword of Vajrakilaya[27] for nine days every year." Later, when Jigme Phuntsok Rinpoche started to give teachings at Nubzur Monastery, it was indeed Lama Tashul who tutored the sangha. In 1926, the year of the fire pig, Tertön Lerab Lingpa's form body dissolved into Dharmadhatu,[28] the expanse of ultimate reality, amid many auspicious signs, and he left his earthly frame and departed to the Copper-Colored Mountain of Glory—the pure realm where Padmasambhava dwells. Lerab Lingpa's Dharma activities then continued into his next life. The terma gateways that he didn't open would be opened by his reincarnation, Jigme Phuntsok Rinpoche. Padmasambhava prophesied:

> The emanation of Lerab Lingpa will be reborn in Kham of
> Tibet,
> And display various manifestations.
> Sometimes he'll manifest as a wise man,
> Inspiring others to develop respect and faith in him;
> Sometimes he'll manifest as a silly individual,
> Giving others the impression of his extraordinariness.
> The states of his body, speech, and mind
> Will be unfathomable to everyone.
> The teachings of Padmasambhava that Lerab Lingpa has
> not propagated
> Will be temporarily guarded by dakinis,
> Waiting to be widely spread by his next incarnation.

PLACE OF BIRTH

The great Jigme Phuntsok Rinpoche was born in a breathtakingly beautiful place called Dzimé Chölhé—the "sacred source of Dharma"—in Dokhok in the Golok region[29] on the Tibetan Plateau. This sacred land has been blessed by many great vidyadharas, including Padmasambhava, and has always been a sphere where the great compassionate Bodhisattva Avalokiteshvara guides and liberates beings. It is surrounded by mountains full of pine trees and colorful flowers. Pure springs burble, melodiously accompanying the songs of hundreds of birds who fly freely in the sky. Fish swim through the pristine waters that gently flow into the Dzimé River. Over a hundred years ago, the great Tertön Wangchuk prophesied Jigme Phuntsok Rinpoche's birth:

> In the vast land of Chölhé,
> Where the illusory demon-subduing lotus flowers blossom everywhere,
> The syllable "HUM" appears in his heart.

Today Jigme Phuntsok Rinpoche's birthplace is marked by a lotus blossom stupa,[30] which was built in 1992 by one hundred monastic members from the Larung Gar Five Sciences Buddhist Academy to commemorate the sixtieth anniversary of Rinpoche's birth.

The Noble Family

In the nineteenth century, the Chakhung family, considered one of the five noble Tibetan families with a long heritage, lived in the sacred land of Dzimé Chölhé. The family heir Chakhung Aten married a virtuous young woman from an esteemed local family, and the couple produced two sons. The eldest son was Dudjom Lingpa (1835–1904), the renowned Dzogchen master and the first Dudjom Rinpoche, who established a retreat center at the sacred Larung Valley where he transmitted tantric teachings. Thirteen of his disciples achieved such a high state of realization there that their physical bodies dissolved into light, a phenomenon known as the "rainbow body." Many other disciples obtained the power of clairvoyance, and the emanations of the Eight Great Bodhisattvas were born as his sons.

The second son, Chakhung Chögyé, had a son named Néchok. Néchok got married and had a son named Chakhung Pété, meaning "lotus." Pété grew into a handsome and outstanding man. He was upright, courageous, sincere, and honest—favorable traits of his heritage. He also attained a certain degree of spiritual realization.

In a place called Nubzur in Sertar, in a family of thirteen consecutive generations of eminent masters, lived a graceful young woman named Yutok, meaning "turquoise lake." She was good-hearted, pure intentioned, fully devoted to the Three Jewels, and compassionate toward others. The local people unanimously praised her outstanding beauty and virtuous characteristics.

Pété and Yutok became a couple and lived together with mutual love and respect. They made a living by herding a small number of cattle and sheep. Despite their frugal lifestyle, they regularly made offerings to the Three Jewels and generously helped the poor. They lived a relaxed and happy life on the Tibetan grasslands.

THE MIRACULOUS BIRTH

In the spring of 1932, at the time of the year when everything starts to wake up again, Yutok was pregnant and experienced many unprecedented feelings. She was in an exceptionally agreeable mood and became more compassionate toward other beings. At the same time, Pété had many auspicious dreams. The couple often smelled a wonderful fragrance inside their tent, which amazed them. Their neighbors constantly heard melodious sound coming from the couple's tent, among many other incredible signs and phenomena.

Yutok gave birth in 1933, on the third day of the first Tibetan month, an auspicious month that celebrates Buddha Shakyamuni subduing the six leaders of the *tirthikas*—proponents of non-Buddhist views. She felt relaxed and cheerful, experiencing no pain at all.

In an ordinary birth, a baby affected by karmic forces is normally born head down. But this child left the mother's womb with his head upright and immediately assumed the vajra posture. He opened his eyes, gazed at people with a smile on his face, threw the placenta over his left shoulder as if it were his Dharma robe, and recited seven times the Manjushri mantra: OM AH RA PA TSA NA DHI.

The people present, including the midwife Drontshe, were in great awe of this miraculous scene. In no time they realized that this was something extraordinary, so they sent messengers to the renowned Pédor Rinpoche. After hearing what had happened, Pédor Rinpoche was very pleased and said, "This child is definitely an incarnation of a great master." Then he admonished everybody: "What just happened is of great importance. You must in no case make it public. To avoid any mishap, please keep it absolutely secret."

Later, based on Lerab Lingpa's prophecy and the extraordinary phenomena at Jigme Phuntsok Rinpoche's birth, Tertön Wangchuk and the great Tulku Pema Norbu (1918–1958) recognized that the newborn was clearly the reincarnation of the great Tertön Lerab Lingpa.

IN HIS MOTHER'S ARMS

After his birth, like any other child, Jigme Phuntsok Rinpoche was nurtured with his mother's breast milk. Yet, unlike other young children who have not yet reached their full cognitive development, he already possessed right views and compassion in his infancy.

In his mother's arms, his big eyes gazed at everything around him. Jigme Phuntsok Rinpoche later recalled that every time during his infancy when he saw someone slaughtering livestock, great compassion arose from his heart, and he would think, "It is a great pity that these innocent beings are being killed. If possible, I would exchange my own precious life for their lives." But, being an infant, he could not express his thoughts in words, so he could only hold on to his mother and cry loudly. This innate *bodhichitta*[31] was present throughout his life: every time he encountered living beings in pain or sorrow, he would think, "How wonderful would it be if I could liberate them from suffering, offer them blessings and happiness, and fulfill all their wishes!"

When he saw images of buddhas or Buddhist scriptures, he would appear very happy, move his hands and feet joyfully, giggle cheerfully, touch them with his soft little hands, and put his palms together in respect. Before he could pronounce "Mama," he could already recite the mantras of Avalokiteshvara and many other deities.

Sometimes his mother put him in his cradle while she went out to work. Through the roof opening of the tent, he could see the green pines on the hills and the clear blue sky. He was amazed with the thought, "How tall these trees are! They've grown into the sky!" He was full of curiosity about the external world.

At the age of three or four, he already had extraordinary devotion to Mipham Rinpoche. In Jigme Phuntsok Rinpoche's mind, Mipham Rinpoche was Bodhisattva Manjushri. When young Jigme Phuntsok Rinpoche prayed to him, he thought he was praying to Manjushri. Because of the extraordinary blessing power of this prayer, it was very common for him to see the appearances of peaceful and wrathful buddhas and bodhisattvas.

If he had a vision of wrathful deities after dusk, he would be very afraid. Thus, before going to bed, he often pleaded with his mother, saying, "Dear mom, please don't fall asleep before me; otherwise, when I see those wrathful bodhisattvas, I will be very scared." His mother gently reassured him, "Don't be afraid. I will always stay by your side. We will fall asleep together." Knowing his mother would stay with him, young Jigme Phuntsok Rinpoche was at ease and gradually fell asleep in the warmth of his mother's arms. As he grew older, his compassion, faith, and desire to learn only grew stronger.

The Blossom of the Wisdom Lotus

Like other children, at the age of six, Jigme Phuntsok Rinpoche started learning to read and write. When he first learned the alphabet, he found it somewhat difficult, so he could not help but feel a bit anxious.

One day, when passing a pile of *mani* stones—stones inscribed with mantras and other Buddhist prayers—at a place called Khanga, Jigme Phuntsok Rinpoche saw a small piece of crumpled paper sticking out of an opening between the rocks. Out of curiosity, he took the paper out. On opening it, he found many words written on it. As he was not yet able to read, he asked someone to recite them for him. It turned out to be *The Sadhana of the Lion of Speech Manjushri*, and at the end of the text was the following verse:

> In the holy land of India, an old man
> At the age of ninety-nine,
> Was illiterate, but through diligent practice,
> He had a vision of Manjushri one day later.

After hearing this, young Jigme Phuntsok Rinpoche thought to himself, "If such an old man could reach a high level of attainment after only one day of practice, a child like me should have no problem succeeding in the practice." He was very happy and clapped his hands, saying, "This is great! This is great!" Thereafter, he wholeheartedly dedicated himself to the practice for a few days, and as a result many auspicious signs of blessing appeared. From that day on, without any further study or effort, Jigme Phuntsok Rinpoche naturally knew how to read and write. In addition, he naturally understood the general contents of all scriptures and commentaries.

The qualities of great masters like Jigme Phuntsok Rinpoche are reflected through their hearing, contemplation, meditation, oral presentation, debate, composition, discipline, concentration, wisdom, and activities of propagating the Dharma and benefiting sentient beings. But many ordinary people are drawn to a master's supernatural abilities and, as is said in the sutra, "the worldly fools develop faith upon [the master's] supernatural power." In light of this, here is a brief account of Rinpoche's supernatural powers shown at the age of five or six.

Jigme Phuntsok Rinpoche had the clairvoyance of divine vision in that he could, for example, see what was obstructed by rocks or mountains; he could read another's mind very clearly; and he could vividly recall the scenes from his previous lives. These scenes included when he was listening to the quintessential teachings of Dzogchen under Padmasambhava, when he was receiving Dzogchen teachings from Lama Shabkar Tsokdruk Rangdrol (1781–1851), when he was attending teachings given by Kongtrul Yönten Gyatso[32] (1813–1899), and especially when he was Dense Yuö Bummé, the son of Denma—the famous minister associated with King Gesar over nine hundred years ago. All these events were still very vivid in his mind, as if they had happened just yesterday.

Due to his activities in his previous life, even as a kid Jigme Phuntsok Rinpoche could already reveal termas as easily as picking something out of a basket. The terma objects he revealed, including Buddha statues and treasure chests holding termas, are still well preserved today at the Larung Gar Five Sciences Buddhist Academy. When hanging out with his friends, Jigme Phuntsok Rinpoche often meditated on the grassland, searching for the coming and going of the mind, and he somewhat recognized the nature of mind. This is similar to what Karma Chakme Rinpoche (1613–1678), one of the most highly realized and accomplished Tibetan meditation masters, did at the age of five. Sometimes during playtime with his friends, he miraculously obtained a terma object.

Moreover, he often had direct visions of deities and *dharmapalas* (Dharma protectors). Lama Lodrö, a well-known master at Dodrupchen Monastery[33] who knew Jigme Phuntsok Rinpoche very well, exclaimed with joy, "So frequently do you encounter deities and dharmapalas! It is either because of the favorable affinity you established in past lives or because of your innate heritage from the Chakhung family. How exceptional!"

COMFORT IN TIMES OF SORROW

When Jigme Phuntsok Rinpoche was only nine years old, his father, who was in his early thirties, passed away. With the loss of their primary breadwinner, his family grew increasingly poor. Jigme Phuntsok Rinpoche's clothes became worn and ragged, and he was frequently bullied by other children.

Once, at a place called Dzongtse near the Five-Colored Lake in Sertar, he was bullied by several children and began to run toward home, crying. It was already quite late by that time, and the sky was covered by thick, dark clouds. It started to rain heavily, and Jigme Phuntsok Rinpoche got caught in the downpour. By the time he arrived home, his clothes were soaking wet. Late that night, young Jigme Phuntsok Rinpoche lay in bed, wrapped in wet clothes and staring out into the darkness. He was unable to sleep. It was still pouring rain outside, with deafening thunder and flashing lightning. He shivered with the cold and felt very sad. Thinking of his loving father who had left him at such a young age, he felt life was full of suffering. With tears rolling down his cheeks, he gradually dozed off into a state that was half-awake and half-asleep.

Jigme Phuntsok Rinpoche had a luminous dream in which Padmasambhava appeared before him with one face, two arms, and one hand in the threatening gesture, shining rays of light, sitting with his legs in the posture of royal ease and smiling. With great compassion, Padmasambhava told Jigme Phuntsok Rinpoche, "Young man, don't be sad, and do not become averse to this world. When you grow up, you will become an extraordinary person and be venerated by many people like the bright moon surrounded by stars. Mipham Rinpoche will take you directly under his care and grant you blessings. Your future Dharma activities will be vast." After comforting him, Padmasambhava disappeared. Jigme Phuntsok Rinpoche was greatly uplifted and inspired. His sorrow and aversion were all gone.

The next day, he woke up feeling recharged and aspired to be diligent. He was full of confidence about his future. At that moment, the eastern sky was filled with the red hues of dawn, and the rising sun slowly revealed its smiling face, seemingly heralding Jigme Phuntsok Rinpoche's glorious Dharma activities to come.

Interesting Childhood Stories

Childhood stories often bring up special feelings, whether they are our own or someone else's. When the child in question is a great spiritual master like Jigme Phuntsok Rinpoche, these stories are even more enchanting. So, here are a few stories collected from his childhood.

Once, Jigme Phuntsok Rinpoche and a few friends were crossing a rushing river. Hand in hand, step by step, they searched for the river floor with their feet. Suddenly, they discovered a big rock in the middle of the river blocking their path. Jigme Phuntsok Rinpoche's friends were visibly afraid and did not know what to do. The four-year-old Jigme Phuntsok Rinpoche calmly said to them, "Do not be afraid. Just follow me!" Then he stepped onto the slippery rock. On the spot where he put his feet, a line of deep and clear footprints was formed, thus creating several depressed parts for the other children to use as steps. Everybody happily followed Jigme Phuntsok Rinpoche and eventually crossed the river. The imprints on the rock are still clearly visible today.

Another time, young Jigme Phuntsok Rinpoche was playing tag with his friend Gendün. At first, the two friends just frolicked with each other. Eventually their playing got rough, and they started wrestling together. Because young Jigme Phuntsok Rinpoche was skinny and not as powerful as the strong Gendün, he was pinned down. Just when Gendün was lifting his hand to strike him, young Jigme Phuntsok Rinpoche cleverly grabbed him by the ears and jerked him up, causing Gendün to cry out in pain. Gendün begged for mercy, "Please let go of me! Please stop pulling my ears. I won't hit you anymore." Then they were friends again, just like before.

It seems common to us that a river flows downward. However, a great accomplished being who has attained the power of freely maneuvering the four elements of earth, water, fire, and air can make a river flow upward. At the age of ten, on a clear summer day, Jigme Phuntsok Rinpoche herded a group of yaks across the Sertar River. The river was calm, and the water level just barely reached his ankles. While the yaks grazed freely on the wide and spacious plain, Jigme Phuntsok Rinpoche lay on the soft grass. As he was gazing at the cloud-dotted blue sky, he started observing the nature of his mind. Slowly, his mind seemed to become one with the empty space, and he entered a state of no-self. As time passed by, he didn't notice that the setting sun had already disappeared below the horizon. Suddenly, fierce winds started blowing, dark clouds engulfed the sky, and a hailstorm hit. As if waking up from a dream, young Jigme Phuntsok Rinpoche emerged from his meditative state, quickly gathered all the yaks, and started herding them back home.

When he reached the Sertar River, he stepped into the water without realizing that the water level had greatly risen. As a result, he was swept away by the current. Seeing this, the people on the shore were shocked and started shouting, "A child has been swept away by the river! Come help quickly!" The bystanders didn't know what to do. They could only sigh helplessly. Suddenly someone cried out, "Look! The river is flowing upward now!" All eyes focused on the river. It is hard to believe, but the water was indeed flowing upward, and it formed a whirlpool, in the middle of which young Jigme Phuntsok Rinpoche was lying peacefully, as if he were still observing the nature of his mind. Everybody was in awe. He eventually reached the shore safely and continued herding his yaks home as if nothing had happened.

Parting with Worldly Life
in the Bloom of His Youth

Even though young Jigme Phuntsok Rinpoche was as mischievous as his friends and sometimes did things that amused adults, he never did anything inconsistent with Buddhist principles.

As time passed, Jigme Phuntsok Rinpoche grew from a bright, joyful child into a smart young man. His disposition became refined and transcendent, and his deep, sharp eyes could see through worldly phenomena. Having witnessed the suffering brought by birth, old age, sickness, and death, there arose in his heart a strong desire for renunciation from the endless suffering of this cycle known as *samsara*. The analogy of "laymen live in the fire pits, and monks live in cool quarters" deeply resonated with him. Although his family expected him to take up the responsibility of continuing the family lineage and making a name for himself in society, he had already made up his mind to leave the mundane world behind.

At the age of fourteen, Jigme Phuntsok Rinpoche gave up everything in his worldly life without the slightest regret. He took his *samanera*, or novice monk, ordination vows in front of Khenpo[34] Sönam Rinchen and was given the monastic name of Thubten Lekshe Zangpo, meaning "Virtue of Eloquence." From that day on, his monastic life revolved around the cultivation of hearing, contemplating, and meditating on the Dharma. He followed many qualified Dharma masters and extensively studied Sutrayana and Vajrayana teachings. He memorized scriptures pertaining to the five principal topics[35] of Buddhism—no fewer than three hundred stanzas per day. His intelligence and wisdom were unstoppable, like a tidal wave. Jigme Phuntsok Rinpoche began giving teachings to fortunate recipients of the Dharma at the same age that the renowned Dzogchen master Longchenpa (1308–1364) started turning the Wheel of Dharma.

During that period, with the wisdom arising from Jigme Phuntsok Rinpoche's pristine awareness, he produced many profound and eloquent works. Unfortunately, excluding *The Sadhana of Mipham Rinpoche Practice*, many of these works were lost, including *The Outer, Inner, and Secret Praise to Manjushri's Sword of Wisdom* and *The Pith Instructions on the Practice of the Eight Eloquences*.

His Extraordinary Wisdom

In his teenage years, Jigme Phuntsok Rinpoche already excelled in wisdom and eloquence. Once, he visited Lama Yukhok Chatralwa Chöying Rangdrol (1872–1952), a renowned master who was considered the emanation of the great eighth-century Dzogchen master Vimalamitra.[36] Lama Yukhok teased him, saying, "I heard that you were quite capable of enduring hardships for the true Dharma and that you lived a poor and simple life. But looking at your rosy cheeks and healthy complexion, I start to doubt what I've heard." He then continued, "I heard that you were the reincarnation of the great Tertön Lerab Lingpa, the eminent master who once gave the Thirteenth Gyalwa Rinpoche the vase empowerment and sprinkled nectar on his tongue.[37] Now you certainly can't do the same. Don't you feel ashamed?"

To refute Lama Yukhok, Jigme Phuntsok Rinpoche adopted the lama's logic of argument and replied, "I heard that you were the emanation of Vimalamitra, who used to give the precious vase empowerment to the second Buddha Padmasambhava and sprinkled nectar on his tongue. Now you certainly can't do the same. Don't you feel ashamed?"

"Who says that I am Vimalamitra's emanation?" Lama Yukhok responded.

"Well then, who says I am the reincarnation of Lerab Lingpa?" Jigme Phuntsok Rinpoche retorted.

Lama Yukhok was unable to refute back. He laughed with joy and raised his thumb, saying, "At this young age, you already have such extraordinary wisdom and eloquence! This is delightful! So admirable!"

Jigme Phuntsok Rinpoche frequently visited the pure realms

with his illusory body in his dreams and received profound teachings from many buddhas and bodhisattvas. Though asleep, he was fully aware of his surroundings, including people and their actions, as if they were in broad daylight. He also possessed the extraordinary ability to foretell the future. This is shown in his writing titled *The Prophecies of the Future*, in which he accurately predicted the murder of Sönam Norbu, an official of Sertar; the destruction of Nubzur Monastery by the army; and many other incidents.

THE COMPLETE REALIZATION
OF DZOGCHEN

Unlike most fifteen-year-olds who still wander aimlessly and haven't found direction in life, Jigme Phuntsok Rinpoche had a mind that had blossomed with the wisdom of hearing, contemplating, and meditating on the Dharma. While extensively studying Sutrayana and Vajrayana, he developed unspeakable faith in the teachings of the ultimate Great Perfection, or Dzogchen. Within a short period of time, he had wholeheartedly recited the following four-verse prayer to Mipham Rinpoche one million times:

> Through the blessings of the youthful Manjushri, the union
>   of awareness and emptiness,
> You released the eight brilliant treasures of eloquence from
>   the expanse of your wisdom mind.
> Master of an ocean of treasure-like teachings of the Dharma
>   in both aspects, transmission and realization—
> To you, Mipham Rinpoche, Manjushri in person, I pray!

He also thoroughly studied and recited ten thousand times Mipham Rinpoche's *Pointing Out the Nature of the Mind*—a work that encompasses the quintessence of Dzogchen's pith instructions. At that time, his mind had been completely transcended. All his ordinary thoughts such as greed, attachment, and duality were wiped out like chaff, and the naked awareness, which is empty and immaculately pure in nature, swiftly emerged. All fetters of dualistic thoughts had dissolved, and he then experienced a profound realization. It is with no exaggeration to say that, even if hundreds and thousands of great achieved masters were to come together and refute his convictions, he would not budge in the slightest.

Mipham Rinpoche, the true emanation of Bodhisattva Manjushri, in his illusory body, took Jigme Phuntsok Rinpoche under his care and bestowed upon him the name Ngawang Lodrö Tsungmé. Vidyadhara Taksham Nüden Dorjé (1655–1708) once prophesied:

> Upholding the Buddha's teachings and mastering the
> meaning of tantras,
> The reincarnation of Nanam Dorjé Dudjom named
> Ngawang
> Will possess mighty power and attain the realization of
> Yamantaka.[38]

Tertön Chöjé Lingpa also made a prediction about this specific sacred name:

> The one named Ngawang, who dresses in maroon robes,
> Will be renowned all over Kham, U-Tsang, and beyond,
> And widely propagate the Sutrayana and Vajrayana
> teachings throughout the ten directions.

Jigme Phuntsok Rinpoche's state of realization at that time was recorded in his *Commentary on Pointing Out the Nature of the Mind*. At the age of sixteen, dwelling in his pristine awareness, he wrote *The Pith Instructions on the Practice of the Great Perfection*.

Although he had reached a high level of enlightenment, to show his followers that true Dharma is precious and hard to encounter and to showcase the importance of following qualified teachers, he continued to properly follow a few qualified teachers as described in the next chapters.

LEAVING HIS HOMETOWN

At the age of sixteen, when Jigme Phuntsok Rinpoche first heard the name of Changma Khenchen Thubten Chöpel, also known as Thubga Rinpoche (1886–1956), he got goose bumps and couldn't help crying. It was just like Milarepa's reaction on hearing the name of Marpa for the first time. Jigme Phuntsok Rinpoche thought to himself, "No matter what, I must go and pay respects to Thubga Rinpoche."

Jigme Phuntsok Rinpoche and his fellow villager Tröpa planned to go to Sershul where Thubga Rinpoche was teaching and follow this great teacher. Unfortunately, Jigme Phuntsok Rinpoche's mother fell ill from overexertion and was bedridden. He could not bear to leave her in this state, so he temporarily set aside his plan.

In the following year, Jigme Phuntsok Rinpoche's mother passed away, which greatly saddened him. He thought to himself, "My father died at a young age, and my mother passed away before reaching an old age. From now on, I desire nothing but the true Dharma. I should go and visit my qualified teacher now."

After his mother's funeral, he started packing for his trip to Sershul and made arrangements with Tröpa to set off. On leaving, Jigme Phuntsok Rinpoche was stopped by a few relatives who were unwilling to let him travel such a far distance. He had no choice but to return to his monastery. He thought, "If we leave in broad daylight, they will find out and stop us again, so we have to leave at night." He then snuck out of the monastery in the dead of night when everyone was sleeping and met up with Tröpa. Together they left their village for Sershul.

The next day, the monks in the monastery found Jigme Phuntsok Rinpoche's bed empty, with only a note on the bedside, stating:

My kind and loving mother has departed from this world,
Causing excruciating pain in my heart.
I deeply realize that all conditioned things
Are as fleeting as lightning,
And that only the illumination of the Dharma
Is trustworthy and dependable.
Now I am leaving my hometown
To follow my lama at another place.
If one day I come back here,
I will undoubtedly benefit you with the shower of Dharma.

Reading the note, the sangha members couldn't help but feel sad about Jigme Phuntsok Rinpoche's departure.

LIFE AT SERSHUL

In those days, traveling was more challenging as there was no easy means of transportation like today. Enduring hunger and cold, Jigme Phuntsok Rinpoche and Tröpa crossed over mountains with their luggage on their backs. When they could no longer continue due to lack of food, they would beg for alms. After numerous hardships, they finally reached Thubga Rinpoche's Buddhist institute at Sershul.

Despite fatigue from the long journey, Jigme Phuntsok Rinpoche immediately went to see Lama Thubga Rinpoche. The lama was a tall man, slim but strong, austere but compassionate, and dressed in worn monk's robes. On seeing Thubga Rinpoche, instantly there arose in Jigme Phuntsok Rinpoche unsurpassable devotion, and all his ordinary thoughts disappeared. He prostrated to the lama right away and silently made a promise, "I shall for the rest of my life follow my lama wholeheartedly with the three ways to please the teacher."[39] Thereafter, he earnestly received the comprehensive Sutrayana and Vajrayana teachings, especially the empowerment, oral transmission, and pith instructions of Dzogchen, from Thubga Rinpoche.

At Sershul, Jigme Phuntsok Rinpoche engaged in meticulous studies just like an ordinary monk. He lived in a ramshackle hut made of hay bales that was only big enough for one person to enter. It was no more than a shelter from wind and rain, and barely that— during storms it would shake and rumble as if it were about to collapse. When it snowed in winter, the hut was totally buried in the snow and became like a pile of snow in the landscape.

No matter what the season or temperature was, all he wore were clothes made of abandoned ragged fabrics he found on the charnel grounds. Normally a young man of eighteen or nineteen years old requires sufficient nutrition for growth; however, Jigme Phuntsok Rinpoche could sustain himself with only the little bit of yogurt that was distributed among the monks. These hardships were similar to what other great teachers had experienced, like Longchenpa when following Rigdzin Kumaradza (1266–1343). The monks of the Buddhist institute at Sershul were greatly impressed by Jigme Phuntsok Rinpoche's ability to endure hardships while following in the footsteps of great teachers in his pursuit of the Dharma.

When Jigme Phuntsok Rinpoche first arrived at the institute, many resident monks did not acknowledge his intelligence and wisdom. Once he engaged in a debate with another monk on a topic of Abhidharma. The debate grew in intensity, and many learned monks joined in to refute Jigme Phuntsok Rinpoche's arguments. Then Jigme Phuntsok Rinpoche brought up a very powerful but rarely quoted statement from *The Great Commentary on Abhidharma*, and the other monks unanimously denied the existence of such scriptural evidence. After leafing through the commentary, the other monks found that Jigme Phuntsok Rinpoche's argument was in fact valid. The monks were totally amazed. From then on, they respected and admired Jigme Phuntsok Rinpoche for his wisdom and learning.

STUDYING THE OCEAN-LIKE TEACHINGS
WITH QUALIFIED TEACHERS

In addition to receiving the Sutrayana and Vajrayana teachings from his root lama Thubga Rinpoche, Jigme Phuntsok Rinpoche studied with the following teachers on the five principal topics of Mahayana Buddhism and other tantric texts:

> From Lama Padma Siddhi, he received the pith instructions on the primordial purity and spontaneous presence of the mind's essential nature, as well as the bardo teachings.
>
> From the great realized master Namkha Jigme, he received the teaching of *Lama Yangtik* (*The Innermost Heart Drop of the Guru*) and the empowerment of the one hundred deities.
>
> From Dzogchen Khenpo Yönten Gönpo (1916–1984), he received the great empowerments of *Nyingtik Yabshyi* (*Four Parts of Heart Essence*) and *Kalachakra*.
>
> With Khenpo Gyatso (1903–1957) he studied Nagarjuna's *Root Verses on the Middle Way*, Aryadeva's *Four Hundred Stanzas on the Middle Way*, Chandrakirti's *Introduction to the Middle Way*, and other texts of the Madhyamika, or the Middle Way school.
>
> With Lama Tséga, he studied the topic of Abhidharma, including the teaching on *The Great Commentary on Abhidharma*, as well as received the full transmission of the Tripitaka.
>
> With Khenpo Orgyen Gönpo, he studied Vinaya, or disci-

pline, including the teachings on *Three Hundred Verses*, the *Dultika*,[40] and others.

With Lhatrul Rinpoche, he studied Maitreya's *Ornament of Clear Realizations* and other common teachings, such as Buddhist logic, astrology, and grammar. Jigme Phuntsok Rinpoche also received teachings from the great yogi Lama Karchö, Tulku Pema Norbu, Khenpo Dawö, Lama Gendün Dargyé, Sönam Rinchen, Lodrö Lozang, Lama Ölo, and many others.

In summary, he followed over ten teachers and received a large number of essential Sutrayana and Vajrayana teachings under their guidance. Jigme Phuntsok Rinpoche followed each of his teachers wholeheartedly with respect, genuineness, and sincerity. Once a disciple pleaded with the great Jigme Phuntsok Rinpoche to write his autobiography, and he replied, "I don't have anything worth writing down except one thing: I have never done anything to upset any of my teachers. I have always treated each of them with utmost respect and followed their instructions. This is the only thing to be put in my biography."

In particular, his faith and devotion to his root lama Thubga Rinpoche was beyond words. Jigme Phuntsok Rinpoche said many times to his disciples and followers: "From the time I first saw my root lama until the day he passed away, I have never for even a second seen him as an ordinary person. My root lama placed great emphasis on upholding disciplines, and his disciples emulate him in this. As it is said in the *Introduction to the Middle Way*:

The ocean and a corpse do not remain together;
Good fortune and calamity do not keep company.
Likewise the great ones, who have perfect discipline,
Decline the company of dissolute behavior.[41]

Therefore, I always believed that he was a second-stage bodhisattva.[42] But, when I witnessed all the auspicious signs at the time of his parinirvana, I then realized that my lama had already attained the ultimate Buddhahood."

Jigme Phuntsok Rinpoche also said:

> During the six years that I had followed Thubga Rinpoche, I have never annoyed him. Just as how Jigme Gyalwai Nyugu (1765–1843) followed his root lama Jigme Lingpa (1730–1798), I haven't done anything that annoyed or dissatisfied my lama. Nevertheless, there was one time when I refused to visit a deceased layman's house and recite for the village ceremony, as I did not want to be distracted from my own study and practice. When Thubga Rinpoche found out, he said to me, "Don't you want to benefit living beings anymore?" I was so nervous and embarrassed that I started to cry. I have never had any negative thought on my lama's actions. Even when he was joking, I still felt the joke had some profound secret meaning, so I would regard it as a supreme teaching. Every time when my lama blessed me by touching my head or putting his forehead against mine, I would be ecstatic for a few days.

While giving teachings to hundreds and thousands of people, the great Jigme Phuntsok Rinpoche would always shed tears whenever he mentioned or recalled Thubga Rinpoche. This shows how deeply he missed his root lama. Whoever has attended Jigme Phuntsok Rinpoche's teaching in person can feel his wholehearted guru devotion.

Going Through Hardships in Pursuit of Dharma

During his time at Sershul, Jigme Phuntsok Rinpoche heard of Lama Padma Siddhi, a renowned Tibetan master who was commonly regarded as an emanation of Avalokiteshvara, or Chenrezik in Tibetan. Thus, the Tibetans called him Lama Chenrezik. Jigme Phuntsok Rinpoche really wanted to visit the lama and ask for his teachings. On a winter day, he shared his plan with Thubga Rinpoche, who readily agreed.

Overjoyed, Jigme Phuntsok Rinpoche shared the good news with his friend Tröpa. Tröpa was very surprised, asking, "Did the lama really give you permission?"

"Yes, he really did. Well then, are you coming with me?" Jigme Phuntsok Rinpoche affirmed.

"Wherever you go, I will definitely accompany you!" Tröpa exclaimed.

Coincidentally, Jigme Phuntsok Rinpoche's Dharma brothers Dargyé and Longsal were also going to visit Lama Chenrezik, so the four of them set off together. The timing of their trip, however, could not have been worse. Due to prolonged heavy snowfall, it had been the hardest winter in over one hundred years in Kham. The whole region had been transformed by the thick, knee-high snow into a desolate place with few traces of human beings. Snowstorms killed many livestock; for instance, an affluent herdsman's family lost almost all their four or five hundred yaks. Many people had no choice but to migrate to places that were not affected by the snowstorms.

During the companions' trip, it kept snowing day and night, so all they could see was a vast and boundless white plain. The four of them struggled to walk in the snow. Every time they put one foot down, they had to use a lot of force to pull the other one out of the snow. They proceeded slowly, covering only one or two kilometers per day. When they got caught by a blizzard, they lost direction and ended up walking in circles for two days without going any farther.

Due to trekking in the snow, two or three layers of skin on their legs peeled off, causing continuous bleeding and searing pain. Jigme Phuntsok Rinpoche thought to himself, "In his previous lives, Buddha Shakyamuni was willing to give up his life for four lines of the true Dharma. Then it is no big deal that I must undertake a little hardship. As it is said, only after a bone-chilling winter do plum blossoms smell the best." With this thought in mind, he was even more determined than before.

Tröpa, however, was on the verge of giving up, so he said wearily, "I don't know when we will finally arrive. Let's just go back!"

Jigme Phuntsok Rinpoche encouraged him, saying, "We have already come this far. If we give up halfway, all the efforts we have already put in will be for nothing. As we haven't received the true Dharma, wouldn't that be a great waste of time? Only when we can endure the unendurable and do the undoable can we be called true practitioners." He then reminded Tröpa of the hardships that Sadaprarudita, Bodhisattva Ever-Weeping, had gone through in seeking the Dharma, notably selling his blood and bone marrow to afford a suitable offering for the bodhisattva Dharmodgata. After hearing this, Tröpa was inspired and uplifted, so he walked forward with his head held high, full of vigor and vitality. Seeing this, the other three could not help but laugh out loud as they continued on their journey.

The only food they had brought was a small amount of *tsampa*, the traditional Tibetan flour made from roasted barley. Tröpa was put in charge of rationing, and he took the task very seriously. If the group hadn't yet become too hungry to walk any farther, Tröpa wouldn't take the tsampa out.

Every time he distributed the tsampa, Tröpa would say, "This is tsampa, and we don't have much. Let's be frugal. Remember that when Buddha Shakyamuni was going through his six years of ascetic practice, he ate only one grain of rice in the first two years, drank one drop of water in the second two years, and had neither food nor water in the last two years. Therefore, we should emulate him." During the whole trip they quenched their thirst only with snow. They slept inside a hole they dug out of the snow at night, and they set out again by dawn the next day.

After many cloudy and snowy days, they were all longing for the sun, but they did not realize that it would bring even more torments. The sun reflecting off the snow hurt their eyes so badly that they could not even keep them open. They managed to walk by taking turns, two by two. Two of them would be the eyes for everyone until they could no longer see, while the other two kept their eyes closed to recover. Then they would switch. In this way they took turns leading the way. Tröpa was distraught and said, "It's better not to have a sunny day. May the lama and the Three Jewels bless us!"

Thankfully, the next day it was cloudy, but the gusts of harsh wind attacked them like a sharp knife piercing their skin. They were freezing and shivering, their teeth chattering. The saliva that dripped from their mouths turned into ice the moment it reached the ground. Tröpa suffered the most of frostbite. He kept clenching his teeth, which made him look as if he were smiling. Seeing this, Jigme Phuntsok Rinpoche immediately said to Longsal and Dargyé, "Tröpa is too cold to move. Let us drag him and run, or he will be in danger." The three of them started running through the snow, dragging Tröpa along. After running a few miles, Tröpa's body gradually warmed up, and he slowly returned to normal.

One day, they had not walked far when several fierce bears aggressively approached them. Tröpa's first reaction was to run away, while Dargyé and Longsal planned to use sticks for self-defense. Jigme Phuntsok Rinpoche said, "None of these techniques will work. We should pray wholeheartedly to Buddha Shakyamuni and Bodhisattva Avalokiteshvara to get rid of their hostility." They then prayed as Jigme Phuntsok Rinpoche suggested. It was indeed effective, and the bears slowly retreated as if they had become compassionate.

On the thirteenth day of the trip, the group saw a human silhouette in the far distance. They thought it might be a bandit. Dargyé said, "Anyhow, at least we've run into another human. It looks like a good sign to me. For more than ten days we walked only through deserted places." That evening, they finally arrived at a snow-free area. They gathered some twigs and branches, built a stove, made a fire, and boiled some tea, and after dinner they had a good sleep.

On the following day, they all felt uplifted and soon arrived at a nearby monastery, where they asked for Lama Chenrezik's residence. After lunch, they immediately headed in that direction. Four or five hours later, they finally got to meet Lama Chenrezik. Jigme Phuntsok Rinpoche requested confirmation regarding his own level of realization, to which Lama Chenrezik attested affirmatively. Lama Chenrezik also offered the group supreme tantric pith instructions.

At the time of their visit, Lama Chenrezik was giving teachings on the benefits of the Avalokiteshvara mantra, and the sangha had been chanting the mantra together. He was also teaching *The Way of the Bodhisattva*, so Jigme Phuntsok Rinpoche and his three travel companions attended one class, in which they heard a few stanzas, such as:

> And though they treat it like a toy,
> Or make of it the butt of every mockery,
> My body has been given up to them.
> Why should I make so much of it?[43]

They were greatly inspired by the teaching. Lama Chenrezik praised Jigme Phuntsok Rinpoche in public, saying, "Because the chief disciple of Thubga Rinpoche has joined us this time, the merits accumulated through our mantra recitation have increased a hundred times." After having received the essential teachings, Jigme Phuntsok Rinpoche and his three friends bid farewell to Lama Chenrezik.

On the way home, when they reached the bank of the Yellow River, the water level had risen and the bridge was damaged by flooding, forcing them to find another way to cross the river. Eventually, after walking for more than ten days, they still had not been able to cross the river and had to return to Lama Chenrezik's place. Jigme Phuntsok Rinpoche said, "On the way here we encountered many hardships, and now on the way back we again encountered many adversities."

Lama Chenrezik reassured them, "Enduring hardships in search of the true Dharma can purify karmic obscurations accumulated throughout your past lives and remove obstacles for your future Dharma activities. You should instead feel delighted." Hearing this, they felt inspired again and set out on their return journey.

By then the snow had started to melt, which brought them new obstacles. Sometimes they got buried by a small avalanche, and it took them a very long time to climb out of the snow. One day while they were walking, more than twenty dogs from a nearby household charged fiercely at them. The three companions were so scared that they were about to run, but Jigme Phuntsok Rinpoche calmly said, "Running is not an option, as we certainly can't outrun the dogs. I have an idea. Let's put our backs together and defend ourselves with sticks." It indeed worked, and the dogs were not able to get close to them. Soon, the dogs were called back by their owner, leaving the four of them safe.

No matter how meticulous Tröpa had been in managing their food consumption, the rest of the tsampa was consumed before the trip was over. Having eaten nothing for two or three days, they were too starved to stand on their feet, so they had to beg for alms. Jigme Phuntsok Rinpoche and Tröpa visited a household where they received a lot of food and were invited inside for lunch. Longsal and Dargyé also approached this family. On seeing them, Tröpa told the family host with an air of importance, "Look! Two great masters who uphold pure precepts and are adorned by excellent characteristics are coming this way. You should treat them well and make offerings to them. In this way, you can accumulate boundless merit." Hearing this, Jigme Phuntsok Rinpoche tried hard to hold back his laughter. Fearing that the host would find out the four of them were traveling together, he secretly urged Tröpa not to talk in such a way. Either the host figured out the situation or he had nothing more to offer, so he gave Longsal and Dargyé only a bit of food without inviting them inside for lunch.

It was already dusk when the travelers finally returned to the Buddhist institute at Sershul. Like a loving parent waiting for her wandering children, Thubga Rinpoche was standing by the door and smiling at them. He waved at Jigme Phuntsok Rinpoche and Tröpa, asking them to come over. They went to see their lama with great joy. Thubga Rinpoche said happily to Jigme Phuntsok Rinpoche, "As it has been such a long time since you left, I was worried that Tröpa had taken you back to Sertar. It's good that you're back now." He put his hand on their heads to bless them, and then said, "It is invaluable that you were willing to go through hardships to receive true teachings. Lama Chenrezik is truly an emanation of Avalokiteshvara, and it is not easy to receive teachings from him."

NOBLE CHARACTERS

Being a good person is the prelude to becoming a good Buddhist. Therefore, it is nearly impossible for a person without good character to attain enlightenment through Buddhist practices.

Jigme Phuntsok Rinpoche's innate kindness and compassion contributed to his deep appreciation for teachings pertaining to moral and ethical topics since childhood. He could not help but feel happy and contemplate carefully when hearing or reading such teachings. Because of this, he cultivated an extraordinary character surpassing that of ordinary people.

During his six years of studies in Sershul, being a kind person with young spirit, vigor, bravery, and curiosity, Jigme Phuntsok Rinpoche had never said anything to intentionally hurt another person's feelings, let alone argued or fought with others. He was always gentle, friendly, respectful to his seniors, and caring for his juniors. He treated everyone with integrity, open-mindedness, authenticity, and compassion. Wherever he was, there was always peace and harmony.

Although his knowledge was as vast as space and his wisdom was unsurpassable and unfathomable, his outer behavior was the same as that of any ordinary monk. He never bragged about his outstanding qualities. Anyone who came in contact with Jigme Phuntsok Rinpoche would exclaim, "I would have never thought that such a great and renowned tulku would be so modest, friendly, and easygoing. He doesn't have even the slightest superiority and arrogance."

At such a young age, Jigme Phuntsok Rinpoche was already calm and collected when interacting with others and dealing with challenges. He did not seek success pertaining to the eight worldly concerns.[44] All he did was devote himself to Dharma activities such as hearing, contemplating, meditating, teaching, debating, and writing. His Dharma peers sincerely praised him, saying, "He is unparalleled in his character and deeds in nonspiritual matters, not to mention his spiritual wisdom and realization." Such a remark is not an exaggeration: the great qualities and exemplary conduct of eminent masters, from ancient to modern times, both in the Tibetan region and other places, are vividly embodied in Jigme Phuntsok Rinpoche.

Under the Loving Care of His Lama

At the age of twenty-two, Jigme Phuntsok Rinpoche realized that the true upholding of Buddha Shakyamuni's teachings was carried out by *bhikkhus*, or fully ordained monks, so he took the full ordination vows in front of Thubga Rinpoche. Jigme Phuntsok Rinpoche had been carefully upholding his vows as if he were protecting his own eyes, even during the ten-year havoc of the 1960s and 1970s.

Although the level of realization of his inner yoga practice would have allowed him to take a consort without question, for the sake of growing the monastic sangha, Jigme Phuntsok Rinpoche decided to set an example by engaging in his Dharma activities as a fully ordained monk. The merit of Jigme Phuntsok Rinpoche's deed is unfathomable, influencing the growing sanghas of ordained monks and nuns in the Tibetan areas.

Thubga Rinpoche, who was highly regarded as an enlightened master by all schools and lineages of Tibetan Buddhism, considered Jigme Phuntsok Rinpoche his one and only heart-son among all his disciples. Thubga Rinpoche often expressed his affection, saying, "Jigme Phuntsok and I have deep karmic connections from past lives. When he leaves me, he will not be at ease even for a single day, just like a child can't bear parting with their mother. I also treat him as if he were my own flesh and blood."

Jigme Phuntsok Rinpoche was sometimes mischievous, though without any ill intention. Once, the chief person-in-charge of the sangha criticized him, saying, "As a tulku, you should set an example for others. If you start breaking rules, how can we expect others to follow you?" Hearing this, Thubga Rinpoche appeared discontented and said, "None of you are qualified to criticize my little tulku, because even eighteen of you put together can be no match to his little finger." He would often tell his monastic disciples with a smile, "It's good enough to emulate my little tulku. Even if he walks on his head, you should copy what he's doing."

Thubga Rinpoche gave individual teachings to Jigme Phuntsok Rinpoche on *Chetsün Nyingtik* (*The Heart Essence of Chetsün*) and many other high tantric teachings. Through mind-to-mind blessings, Jigme Phuntsok Rinpoche realized the ultimate wisdom mind of his root lama. His mind and his lama's wisdom had then become one.

Not long after, Nubzur Monastery sent a representative to Sershul to invite Jigme Phuntsok Rinpoche back to assume the position of abbot. Thubga Rinpoche said to the person with a touch of sadness, "Of course, your monastery has the right to decide whether he stays or leaves, since he is your tulku. But our lama-disciple bond is so strong that I will be very sad if he leaves me so abruptly. Please allow us to stay together for one more year. As I only have the lifespan of an old sheep now, you can have him back when I pass away." Thus, Thubga Rinpoche did not consent to letting Jigme Phuntsok Rinpoche return to his monastery.

Time flew by, with one year passing in a flash. The day before Thubga Rinpoche's parinirvana, he called Jigme Phuntsok Rinpoche to his side and said to him with great sincerity, "Last year, when your monastery sent someone to take you back, I couldn't agree to letting you go. But now you and I have no choice but to part ways. In the future, you must devote yourself wholeheartedly to the propagation of the Dharma for the benefit of all living beings. Please pray to me often, and I will grant you blessings." Each of his words was filled with love and compassion for Jigme Phuntsok Rinpoche. Thubga Rinpoche's Dharma activities in this lifetime were perfectly accomplished, and amid numerous auspicious signs his physical body eventually merged into the all-pervading expanse of Dharmadhatu.

Still vividly remembering his ecstasy at first meeting Thubga Rinpoche, Jigme Phuntsok Rinpoche had to endure the excruciating pain of losing his root lama. With this feeling in his heart, he left Sershul, where the true Dharma flourished, and returned to Sertar.

REFUSAL TO TAKE A CONSORT

After six years of studies at Sershul, Jigme Phuntsok Rinpoche returned to Nubzur Monastery at the age of twenty-four. His return brought unprecedented vitality to the monastery, and people were overwhelmed with joy. They arranged a grand enthronement ceremony for him, and from that day on Jigme Phuntsok Rinpoche presided over the monastery and turned the Wheel of Dharma.

One day, a charming young lady called Chöyingma, meaning "Mother of Dharmadhatu," came to Jigme Phuntsok Rinpoche. She was breathtakingly beautiful and elegant, with clear skin and a healthy complexion, like a precious jewel. Though wearing no jewelry or accessories, she appeared noble and immaculate. Her manners were graceful and dignified. She said to Jigme Phuntsok Rinpoche, "I am a dakini with perfect qualities. You and I have strong karmic connections from our past lives. If you accept me as your consort, it will bring great benefit to your Dharma activities."

Jigme Phuntsok Rinpoche thought to himself, "A consort who possesses perfect qualities is of vital importance to a tantric vidyadhara who has transcended the eight worldly concerns. As stated in the *Root Tantra on the Wrathful*, 'Of all illusions, the illusory female is the most extraordinary.' Nevertheless, during the time of the five degenerations,[45] many mundane individuals without any spiritual realization use tantric practice as a pretext to conduct their so-called *consort yoga* for their self-serving desire and lust, which severely defiles the three sets of Buddhist disciplines.[46] To put an end to this wrongdoing, I should uphold the image of a pure monk to propagate the Sutrayana and Vajrayana teachings." With this in mind, Jigme Phuntsok Rinpoche declined Chöyingma's request.

The great Jigme Phuntsok Rinpoche, 1964.
This is the first photo of Rinpoche ever taken.

Chöyingma stayed in the monastery for another two or three days and did everything she could to persuade Jigme Phuntsok Rinpoche to change his mind. But Jigme Phuntsok Rinpoche firmly held to his decision, treating her coldly and ignoring her presence. Finally, realizing it was impossible to sway his decision, Chöyingma sighed and said, "Since you have made up your mind and are not giving me any opportunity, I won't insist any more. But you may regret it one day." After saying this, she left the monastery.

Later, Jigme Phuntsok Rinpoche told Lama Lodrö what had happened. Lama Lodrö said regretfully, "Tibetans have so little merit! Your refusal to accept her as your consort will have a great negative impact on your future Dharma activities, especially on revealing termas. However, if you frequently recite the dakini mantra and praise the merits of consort yoga and subjugating activities[47] in large gatherings, you will still be able to gather many followers in your later years, and your Dharma activities will be vast. At that time, you can widely propagate the teachings of Longchenpa and Mipham Rinpoche." On hearing these words, Jigme Phuntsok Rinpoche remained silent.

The reason Lama Lodrö expressed such regret is because of what had been prophesied by Padmasambhava:

> When he is twenty-six or -seven years old,
> There will be a dakini with all the qualities,
> Known as Nectar Mother of Dharmadhatu,
> Who will urge him to take her as his consort.
> If he is willing to accept her,
> He will be able to open
> Five gateways of the most profound termas,
> And dispel the turbulences in Tibet.
> The brilliant sun will rise high,
> And people will enjoy immense happiness.

The time mentioned in the prophecy had arrived, but because of the Tibetan people's lack of merit, Jigme Phuntsok Rinpoche refused to take the consort. Had he done so, the Land of Snows might have been spared the upheavals that were to occur later.

TEACHING AMID THE SOUND OF GUNFIRE

In 1959, when the great Jigme Phuntsok Rinpoche was twenty-six years old, due to beings' collective karma, the Tibetan region underwent radical upheavals and appalling warfare. Many Tibetan places were in a disastrous state; people lost their homes and were devastated. What was even more dreadful was the destruction of Buddhism. Monasteries were either forced to close or destroyed. Some Buddhist masters were imprisoned, some had to migrate to another country, and some experienced an untimely death. The pure Land of Snows, where Buddhism had been flourishing, was devastated by the horrendous disaster, causing immense suffering and loss. In this unbearable time of war and chaos, how was it even possible to teach the Dharma?

Nevertheless, Jigme Phuntsok Rinpoche managed to give teachings. In a quiet place called Senge Yangdzong, meaning "Lion's Roar Fortress," that was surrounded by army camps, he built a makeshift hut where he persisted in teaching Longchenpa's *Seven Treasures* and other Sutrayana and Vajrayana texts to over sixty of his disciples daily. The rocks near the hut, like fierce lions, formed a fortress; the dense forest became a shield. Very often the practitioners heard gunfire and saw bullets landing next to them or in the trees, causing leaves to scatter. But Jigme Phuntsok Rinpoche always appeared at ease and continued with his teachings, undisturbed.

His disciples reacted differently. Those with meditative capacity and fervent devotion followed the example of their lama and remained focused on the teachings. Those with unsettled, wandering minds were nervous and frightened. It was truly amazing that, although the nearby troops patrolled back and forth, day and night, they never spotted the scene of Jigme Phuntsok Rinpoche giving teachings.

During this period, one day in a dream Jigme Phuntsok Rinpoche came to the Copper-Colored Mountain of Glory in his illusory body and attended a *tsok*, or feast offering, at the Palace of Lotus Light with tens of thousands of dakinis and vidyadharas. Later, he went to the splendid Immeasurable Palace of the West, where he met Padmasambhava and many vidyadharas. Many *dakas*[48] and dakinis happily performed graceful vajra dances and sang melodious vajra songs to welcome Jigme Phuntsok Rinpoche's arrival. Padmasambhava praised his great deeds of teaching the Dharma amid the sound of gunfire.

The most renowned tune for vajra songs at the Larung Gar Five Sciences Buddhist Academy today is the one that Jigme Phuntsok Rinpoche heard at the Copper-Colored Mountain of Glory.

Blessings of the Dharma Protectors

The political situation worsened day by day until it couldn't get any worse. The government authorities directed the demolition of Buddhist statues, defaming the Three Jewels, and the like. At that time, large- and small-scale "struggle sessions"[49] took place all day long; society was in great turmoil, and people were in extreme distress.

Some weak-willed monastics could not withstand the inhumane torture and various forms of humiliation, so they abandoned their monastic vows and chose to disrobe. Some even openly slandered their lamas and the Three Jewels. In Sertar alone, more than eight hundred monks disrobed and renounced their monastic vows to spare their own lives. It was almost impossible to find anyone in monastic attire in the region.

One day, near the end of a struggle session held in the town of Dzichung, a local official spoke sternly: "We have achieved significant results in our recent work. Many monks have changed their position. At tomorrow's meeting, Jigme Phuntsok must speak in public and openly accuse the fault of monastics. If he dares to say something inappropriate, just wait and see what will happen to him!" This threat sent chills down everyone's spine, but Jigme Phuntsok Rinpoche remained calm as if nothing had happened.

Back in his lodging, he thought to himself, "If I refuse to do what they want, my life will be in danger. No matter what, I will never do or say something that brings harm to the Three Jewels, even if I have to give up my life." He then started to make *torma*[50] offerings and pray to the dharmapalas. In the latter part of the night, he felt his face swelling up. In the early morning, Jigme

Phuntsok Rinpoche called in someone, who was startled upon seeing his swollen face. Jigme Phuntsok Rinpoche asked him, "How swollen is my face?"

The other answered, "It is so swollen that your eyes are just slits now. I can barely tell this is you!"

"Very well. May you go and invite one of the local officials over?"

Not long after, an arrogant official walked into Jigme Phuntsok Rinpoche's room. The official was also startled upon seeing him, and stuttered, "How . . . how could he get so sick? Be quick! Have someone take him back to his hometown." Just like that, Jigme Phuntsok Rinpoche defused the crisis.

Whenever a similar situation arose, Jigme Phuntsok Rinpoche would pray particularly to King Gesar and other dharmapalas. His face would then swell up, making him unrecognizable. As a result, he was never forced to speak negatively about the Three Jewels. When recalling what happened at that time, Jigme Phuntsok Rinpoche remarked, "In those special times, it was all thanks to the blessing of the dharmapalas, mainly that of King Gesar and Ekajati,[51] that I was able to skillfully uphold my vows and overcome challenges. Ekajati has never left my side and is always there when I call on her."

In those days, a person would run into disastrous trouble if they were found privately possessing Buddhist scriptures, holding a *mala*—a loop of prayer beads—or spinning a prayer wheel, let alone teaching the Dharma. Once, several local officials, through dirty tricks, confiscated Jigme Phuntsok Rinpoche's work *The Sadhana for the King Gesar Practice* from one of his disciples. They were confident that this evidence would get Jigme Phuntsok Rinpoche into trouble. However, before they were able to do anything, the book disappeared and was miraculously returned to Jigme Phuntsok Rinpoche's bookshelf. Thanks to the blessing of the dharmapalas, the local officials' plot failed once again.

Exempted from Imprisonment

The Land of Snows was mutating to a place of excruciating misery with no sign of relief. The perpetrators, driven by their karmic forces, became increasingly haughty and brutal in persecuting Buddhists. During a riotous struggle session at a place called Rakor, some Buddhists were branded on their bodies with a burning-hot iron, making a horrifying sizzling sound; they could not help but scream aloud from the agonizing burns inflicted on them. Some Buddhists had their heads pressed into a blazing fire. Some were forced to slaughter yaks with a knife. Some were tied together with ferocious dogs. Such atrocities were numerous and hard to describe. The Tibetan region had become a living hell.

Anyone who was spotted wearing any maroon- and yellow-colored robe—the color of the *kasaya*, or monastic robe—was put in prison, let alone anyone wearing a kasaya itself. Nevertheless, the great Jigme Phuntsok Rinpoche continued to wear his monastic robe under his outerwear.

There was a wicked man of the worst kind, who was unscrupulous, overbearing, and hated by everyone. One day, he came to Jigme Phuntsok Rinpoche, clearly without good intentions. He scanned Jigme Phuntsok Rinpoche from head to toe and noticed that he was still wearing the monastic robe. The ill-intentioned man was over the moon, thinking, "This time I can really score big." He ran straightaway to a local official and reported it with exaggerated details. The officials immediately held an emergency meeting to initiate an investigation. At the meeting, the wicked man was insufferably full of himself, believing that he would be rewarded for reporting the alleged "crimes" of Jigme Phuntsok Rinpoche. The investigation, however, quickly turned on the wicked man instead. The illegal deeds he committed in the past were uncovered, so he himself was jailed in the end.

There was a local official who also disliked Jigme Phuntsok Rinpoche and always tried to find fault with him. One day, the official visited Nubzur Monastery and spoke in a sinister manner, "Jigme Phuntsok, it seems that you are a very capable man because you haven't suffered any physical torture yet. But don't feel complacent too early! Today you must clearly tell me, 'Buddhism is a system of superstitions. I now give up the Three Jewels!' Otherwise, I'll give you a hard time."

Jigme Phuntsok Rinpoche replied in a dignified manner, "It is harder than climbing to the sky to make me say so. Buddhism is a completely true faith, and I will never abandon the Three Jewels."

The official became furious and yelled at the top of his lungs, "How dare you to openly speak these words! You are asking for trouble!"

Jigme Phuntsok Rinpoche remained calm and said, "Even if it costs me my life, I will never abandon the Three Jewels."

The official's face turned red, and he pointed at Jigme Phuntsok Rinpoche, shouting, "Alright then! You are truly obstinate! Let's wait and see whether you can still stay nicely in this monastery, or you will be put in prison three days from now! I guess you won't live much longer." Then he stormed off in a rage.

On the way back to Sertar, the official, who had drinking problems, took one drink after another. He became blind drunk but continued to drink. Eventually, he started vomiting blood and died of binge drinking. As he intended to harm a sublime being, he probably ended up suffering in a hell realm three days later.

On another occasion, a person found out that Jigme Phuntsok Rinpoche kept Buddhist scriptures with him and secretly practiced Dharma, so he reported it to the local government. The officials immediately sent a team of soldiers to arrest Jigme Phuntsok Rinpoche, thinking they could finally get him. But, when the team arrived at the valley of Gyopu where Jigme Phuntsok Rinpoche's tent stood, they could find nothing but marks of the removed tent.

After a thorough search, they could not find him anywhere and were forced to leave empty-handed.

Later, when they found out that Jigme Phuntsok Rinpoche had never moved his tent, they were in awe and dared not give him trouble anymore. They also started to watch their language and manners in front of him. The local officials who were aware of this miraculous event are still bewildered when talking about it now.

In His Luminous Dreams

Ordinary people are overwhelmed by discursive thoughts while awake, let alone in their dreams. This is not the case with great Buddhist masters who have fully realized the Great Perfection. Although on the surface there seems to be a distinction between their wakefulness and sleep, they constantly abide in the state of the ultimate luminosity. In other words, for them there is no difference between being awake and being asleep.

In 1970, the year of the iron dog, on the fourteenth day of the ninth Tibetan month, Jigme Phuntsok Rinpoche met the great Tertön Ratna Lingpa (1403–1478) in a luminous dream. The great tertön smiled at Jigme Phuntsok Rinpoche and said, "You should write down everything about the encounter you recently had with King Gesar, so that people can benefit from it. The vajra song that Dakini Neuchung sang at the time carries extraordinary blessing power, so it is of great benefit to anyone who sings it." As we learned from a previous chapter, in one of Jigme Phuntsok Rinpoche's previous lives over nine hundred years ago, he was Dense Yuö Bummé, whose father was Minister Denma and whose consort was Dakini Neuchung.

Heeding Ratna Lingpa's advice, Jigme Phuntsok Rinpoche wrote down his exceptional meeting and included it in his collective works. The following is an excerpt from his writing, which hopefully you will also appreciate:

> On the twenty-fifth day of the seventh Tibetan month in the earth bird year of 1969, I started to practice *The Guru Yoga of King Gesar*. Having been practicing it for

a few days, I entered a luminous dream state in the early morning of the seventh day.

I arrived at the front gate of a palace built of precious jewels. A lovely maiden appeared in front of me. She had rosy cheeks, bright eyes, and white teeth. She was dressed in a purple-red *chuba*, a traditional Tibetan robe, and adorned with distinctive Tibetan jewels such as nine-eyed *dzi* beads and blood coral—a typical look for a Khampa girl. She approached me and happily took my hand, saying, "My close and dear friend, I am so delighted to see you here! I am Neuchung. Have you recognized me? Let's go to your father Denma!" She then held my hand and started walking. We chatted and laughed heartily along the way.

I was enchanted by the conversation with Neuchung and didn't notice that we had already arrived at a majestic palace. We entered a bright and spacious hall, in the middle of which sat a hale and hearty old man who had bright eyes and was dressed in a Tibetan black lamb-fur coat. He reached for the sword placed next to him and forcefully pulled it out from its sheath, causing sparks to fly.

As soon as I saw this old man, I had a strong feeling that he was Minister Denma. Feeling ecstatic, I buried my face in his arms and couldn't help but cry with joy. He gently caressed my head and said, "My beloved son, let's go together to see King Gesar, the embodiment of buddhas of the past, present, and future."

The three of us then came to the Immeasurable Palace made of ruby, inside of which were numerous Buddhist scriptures, Buddha statues, and a variety of provisions. King Gesar was seated on layers of soft cushions, radiant with joy. In his right hand, which rested in the air, he held a five-pronged vajra decorated with colorful ribbons, and in his left hand was a glowing, blue wish-fulfilling jewel. He was wearing a half-moon-shaped cloak and looked majestic. I couldn't clearly remember the other pieces of his clothing.

Upon seeing him, I couldn't help but generate incomparable faith and devotion. I prostrated to him, then put my head on his knees and pleaded, "Dear great master, may all the qualities of your body, speech, and mind merge into me! Please grant me your blessings so that I can widely propagate the Dharma and benefit beings." King Gesar nodded with a smile. Then he waved his vajra in the air and recited the Seven-Line Prayer:

HUM!
In the northwest of the land of Oddiyana,
In the heart of a lotus flower,
Endowed with the most marvelous attainments,
You are renowned as the "Lotus-born,"
Surrounded by many hosts of dakinis,
Following in your footsteps,
I pray to you: Come, inspire me with your
    blessing!
GURU PEMA SIDDHI HUM

He then continued:

As you[52] have now descended to this auspicious
    place,
Please bestow upon us, your disciples, the four
    empowerments,
And grant us the ordinary and extraordinary
    accomplishments.

Then King Gesar put his vajra on the crown of my head. In no time, all my discursive thoughts disappeared into the Dharmadhatu, and the realization of great luminosity and emptiness arose in me.

At that moment, Minister Denma was seated solemnly on a square-shaped Tibetan carpet. Many offerings spontaneously appeared, and we started to make tsok offerings. With her melodious voice, Neuchung sang us a beautiful vajra song. After the song, she softly said to me, "Let's go!" As the two of us were about to leave, I woke up from the dream.

The vajra song that Neuchung sang at that time is included in Jigme Phuntsok Rinpoche's collective works.

HIS TRUE NATURE OF
GREAT COMPASSION

In the turbulent years, people not only underwent spiritual torments but also faced precarious living conditions and shortages of necessities. To make things worse, famines struck the Land of Snows one after another, causing many people to starve to death. It was as if the entire Tibetan region had become a land of hungry ghosts.[53]

Many starving people had no choice but to kill animals for food. Even some Buddhists chose to put aside their precepts and do the same thing. Nevertheless, the great Jigme Phuntsok Rinpoche never hurt a single living being, let alone killed it. As said by Sakya Pandita (1182–1251),

> The wise, no matter how desperate their circumstances are,
>   will never tread the path of the fool,
> Just as a swallow, though thirsty, will never drink from
>   water on the ground.

In those days, it was rare to find someone who still maintained noble conduct. It may not be hard to uphold one's principles and live in accordance with the Dharma when peace is present, but it is truly rare and precious if a person can maintain love and compassion for all beings when faced with great challenges and difficulties. Jigme Phuntsok Rinpoche once said, "Even during those hard times, I had never committed wrongdoings such as killing and stealing. When I was in urgent need of provisions, I would pray to Jambhala, God of Wealth, then I could easily get what I needed.

Sometimes, I would apply the method of extracting essences[54] so I could fast for over ten days." He told his disciples,

> Since my childhood until now, I have never intentionally hurt or killed any living being. But I might have accidentally caused the death of two animals when I was still a young kid. Once, I was sleeping in my tent when a lamb insisted on sleeping with me, so I simply threw it outside. A few days later the lamb died, which made me very sad. The other time, I had to separate a pair of fighting goats with a wooden stick, and I accidentally injured one of them. Later, that goat also died. I suspect that I've caused the two deaths, although I didn't have any intention to do so. Other than that, I have been as loving and kind as possible to living beings throughout my life and have tried my very best to save lives.

Even seeing an animal being killed by others was too unbearable for Jigme Phuntsok Rinpoche. He felt great empathy for the animal. Every time he saw someone beating hungry dogs, he would shed tears and say, "Ever since beginningless time, these beings have been our mothers. Sadly, owing to their karmic debts, they were reborn as animals in this life. They are already so miserable, yet you still beat them without mercy. I'd rather you beat me instead." Once when Jigme Phuntsok Rinpoche witnessed a dog being beaten, an unbearably intense compassion arose in him, and he manifested being sick.

There was another incident in which Jigme Phuntsok Rinpoche saved one of his disciples by transferring poison from the disciple to his own body. Once, a monk called Kunlo was sound asleep at night when a venomous snake crawled under his blanket and bit him twice on the foot. The pain woke him, causing him to sit up abruptly, which scared the snake away. The next morning, when Jigme Phuntsok Rinpoche learned about this, he immediately had someone blow a conch shell, and the whole sangha gathered to recite the specific verses in *Praises to the Twenty-One Taras* that help protect against snake poisons. Meanwhile, Jigme Phuntsok Rinpoche applied other therapeutic treatments to Kunlo, but there was no noticeable improvement. Nobody could think of what else to do. Then Jigme Phuntsok Rinpoche said kindly, "Let me see if there is something else I can do."

The next morning when Kunlo woke up, he felt no more pain in his foot, which amazed him. He sat up and noticed that his wound had disappeared without leaving any trace. Kunlo was so happy that he almost jumped up. Meanwhile, Jigme Phuntsok Rinpoche's right foot became severely swollen in exactly the same spot where Kunlo had been bitten, and there were also snakebite marks. Jigme Phuntsok Rinpoche appeared sick for fifteen days. The sangha knew that he had transferred the snake poison to himself and bore the pain by himself instead.

True compassion and loving-kindness can move heaven and earth. Have you ever seen mice and cats happily play together? Similar to Thogme Zangpo's (1295–1369) life story, many animals that are by nature enemies to each other lived harmoniously around Jigme Phuntsok Rinpoche. For instance, weasels befriended venomous snakes, dogs and wild rabbits got along with each other, and goats and jackals walked side by side. Moreover, Jigme Phuntsok Rinpoche's loyal little dog often risked its own life to save marmots. The reason these animals, who were natural enemies to each other, could live in great harmony is that they were transformed by Jigme Phuntsok Rinpoche's love and compassion.

WHITE LOTUS IN MUDDY WATER

For many years, the Land of Snows suffered unprecedented calamities. It was rare to see someone who could keep the right Buddhist views, continue to teach and practice the Dharma, and not break even the most peripheral branch vows. Yet Jigme Phuntsok Rinpoche was like a white lotus in muddy water, remaining untainted and resolute. While people were put in prison merely for reciting the Avalokiteshvara mantra once, let alone for practicing the true Dharma, Jigme Phuntsok Rinpoche still managed to bestow empowerments, give teachings, and offer pith instructions to fortunate disciples, as well as guide their meditation practice.

With his skillful means and the blessings of the dharmapalas, Jigme Phuntsok Rinpoche taught the Dharma to his disciples in mountain caves and pine forests, often at night by moonlight. In the forest at Dzichen, he transmitted the *Guhyagarbha Tantra* to Khenpo Chöpa and others; in a mountain cave he instructed Khenpo Zabsang and others on *Finding Comfort and Ease in the Nature of Mind*; in a cave at the Gyopu Valley he taught Khenpo Rakho and others *The Way of the Bodhisattva*. As such, Jigme Phuntsok Rinpoche transmitted different Dharma teachings to his disciples in accordance with their different levels of capacity. It was truly rare to find anyone else who could continue to teach the Dharma during the turmoil.

Once, a yogi named Dargyé risked his life to hide Jigme Phuntsok Rinpoche's precious works, such as *The Commentary on Pointing Out the Nature of the Mind*, along with other Buddhist scriptures, in a cave to prevent them from being burned. A few years later, when the scriptures were retrieved, only Jigme Phuntsok

Rinpoche's works were found intact; all the other scriptures were badly damaged by the rain.

Back then, almost all monastics were forced to renounce their vows and practice herding or farming with laypeople. Monastics who still upheld their pure vows were as scarce as stars at dawn. Many people's minds had become so distorted that they even considered it an honor to transgress vows. How very absurd! Many monks gave up their celibacy, but Jigme Phuntsok Rinpoche, despite his charisma and good looks, never paid attention to female advances. Khenpo Gakdor, who used to always be with Jigme Phuntsok Rinpoche like a shadow, remarked with great admiration, "Not to mention breaking vows, he had not even stopped wearing his monastic robe! Today's young people cannot imagine how hard it was in those days to uphold pure vows!"

Jigme Phuntsok Rinpoche once said to his sangha, "Back then, if I had renounced my monastic vows and disrobed, I would be commended and awarded by the government officials. It seemed that there was no one left who was in favor of upholding monastic vows. But, whenever I reflected on how hard it is to have a precious human life, and that discipline is the root of all merit, I would, despite all the hardships, be sternly determined to always uphold my vows as if I am protecting my eyes. Nowadays, we have much more favorable conditions for upholding our vows."

THE MONUMENTAL REVIVAL
OF BUDDHISM

The upheavals devastated Buddhism in the Tibetan region. Monasteries had their roofs or walls dismantled and, in serious cases, were completely leveled to the ground. Buddhist statues and stupas were mutilated or reduced to ruins. Buddhist scriptures were set on fire. Buddhist followers were left with serious wounds or died in jail as a result of inhumane tortures. There was not even one sangha or Buddhist community left intact at that time. The Land of Snows where Buddhism used to flourish had turned into a demonic world. Buddhism was completely paralyzed.

At this critical moment, Jigme Phuntsok Rinpoche, with his extraordinary vigor, acted as a mighty pillar and fearless torchbearer to revive and reinvigorate Buddhism in the Tibetan region. The victory banner of the Dharma was rehoisted, and Buddhism took root again. The revival of Buddhism was a gargantuan task, as it resulted in constant tension with individuals involved in anti-Buddhist activities during the upheavals and with local political leaders. Despite facing numerous challenges, Jigme Phuntsok Rinpoche managed to gather a small group of fully ordained monks at Mount Garuda near Larung Gar to discuss how to revive Buddhism. Then he organized Vinaya ceremonies to transmit samanera and bhikkhu precepts to anywhere from several dozen monks to over a thousand. The number of monastics kept growing. Thus, the *pratimoksha* vows, or the vows of individual liberation, that had nearly disappeared in the preceding years were reintroduced and carried again. Jigme Phuntsok Rinpoche also bestowed the four-arm Manjushri empowerment and gave the Sutrayana and

Vajrayana teachings to the sangha. As such, he revitalized Buddhism. As Padmasambhava prophesied, "At that time, the Tibetan region will slightly resume happiness."

A similar prophecy was made one hundred years ago by the first Dudjom Rinpoche in his *Future Prophecies*:

> A hundred years from now,
> The Dharma will remain merely in name.
> After a certain period of time,
> At the sacred mountain Tsari[55] in Kham,
> The emanation of Nanam Dorjé Dudjom,
> Will rehoist the victory banner of the Dharma.
> If the torch of lineage can be lit,
> The Nyingma teachings will be ever more glorious.

The terma revealed by Tertön Dribdral Rigpé Dorjé says:

> Buddhism temporarily experiences setbacks,
> But will revive one day in Sertar.
> The great eminent master whose name contains "Ah"
> Will become the Dharma King of this place.

Today, the Sutrayana and Vajrayana teachings, especially the Vinaya, can continue to be transmitted and passed on in an unbroken and pure lineage in the Tibetan region. This is thanks to the great Jigme Phuntsok Rinpoche's indefatigable efforts during the turmoil. To commemorate his revival of Buddhism, Jigme Phuntsok Rinpoche's disciples built a Manjushri hall on the summit of Mount Garuda.

THE GOLDEN GARUDA SOARING HIGH

Having gone through fire and water, Jigme Phuntsok Rinpoche's ambition to benefit beings hadn't diminished even a little bit, and he was becoming more motivated and determined. Now that peace had gradually returned, it was time for Buddhism to flourish again. On an auspicious Guru Rinpoche Day—the tenth day of a Tibetan month in 1980, the year of the iron monkey—it was sunny, with auspicious clouds dotting the blue sky. A festive atmosphere seemed to be permeating everywhere. On that day, the Larung Gar Five Sciences Buddhist Academy was inaugurated by the great Jigme Phuntsok Rinpoche in the beautiful valley of Larung. He formally hoisted the victory banner of Buddhism and began his ever-thriving, glorious Dharma activities.

The landscape of the Larung Valley is quite extraordinary. Following the winding mountain road to the academy complex, visitors are in awe of the view. They may feel so inspired and uplifted that they wonder whether they are in the Pure Land of the West.[56] When looking around, they notice that the undulating peaks resemble a blooming six-petaled lotus flower. There are a total of five major peaks in the area, which are called the "little Mount Wutai,"[57] meaning little Five-Peaked Mountains, by the sangha members at Larung Gar. More than one hundred years ago, the first Dudjom Rinpoche established a tantric retreat site with over one hundred huts here. Thirteen of his disciples attained rainbow body in this very valley. Later, this place gradually became deserted.

One day in the 1960s, when Jigme Phuntsok Rinpoche was bestowing the empowerment of the *Guhyagarbha Tantra* on Khenpo Gakdor and a few other disciples, he said, "Thirteen years from now, I am going to establish a Buddhist academy in the Larung Valley. The academy will have many retreat huts, built row upon row, on both sides of the valley. At that time, will you go in for study and contemplation, or for meditation?" Back then, Jigme Phuntsok Rinpoche had already envisioned and planned the academy that appears today.

Tulku Ngedon Chökyi Nyima prophesied in *The Profound Treasury of Lotus*:

> In the magnetizing valley the lotus will bloom,
> The golden garuda of Nubzur will soar high in the air,
> His resounding voice will reach the ten directions,
> And many birds will gather under his wings.

"In the magnetizing valley the lotus will bloom" refers to the lotus-shaped Larung Valley, where magnetizing activities are spontaneously accomplished. "The golden garuda of Nubzur" refers to the great Jigme Phuntsok Rinpoche by his zodiac animal, the bird. "Many birds" refers to his many followers.

As it is also stated in Rigdzin Düden Dorjé's prophecy:

> The sound of Dharma drums in Sertar will shatter heaven and earth.
> The melodious sound of the divine music will attract bees from all directions to gather at this place.

Indeed, ever since Jigme Phuntsok Rinpoche established the academy, disciples have been rushing to Larung Gar from all directions like tidal waves. Starting with just over ten members, the sangha community has grown tremendously since. Now, Larung Gar Five Sciences Buddhist Academy is the largest Buddhist institution in the world.

"I seek no happiness for myself and strive to free all beings from suffering"—this has always been Jigme Phuntsok Rinpoche's aspiration. Therefore, he developed vast bodhichitta, and widely accepted disciples and trained them.

The Larung Gar Five Sciences Buddhist Academy in the early 1980s.

At Larung Gar, Jigme Phuntsok Rinpoche developed a curriculum that covered Sutrayana and Vajrayana teachings, built on his tireless turning of the Wheel of Dharma over the previous decades. In terms of Sutrayana teachings, Jigme Phuntsok Rinpoche primarily expounded on the five principal topics of Mahayana Buddhism; in terms of Vajrayana teachings, he taught the tantric texts

The Larung Gar Five Sciences Buddhist Academy, 1994.

pertaining to the Practice Series[58] and the Dzogchen pith instructions. As a result, he successfully trained many qualified teachers who are now important holders of the Dharma; many of his learned disciples are blowing the Dharma conch and beating the Dharma drum all over the world to benefit beings.

Many of Jigme Phuntsok Rinpoche's disciples have attained true realization and manifested signs of enlightenment. For example, Lama Gochen, who received Jigme Phuntsok Rinpoche's tantric teaching of *Yeshe Lama*, realized the full rainbow body. As mentioned in *The Brief Stories on the Rainbow Body Attainment in Vajrayana*,[59] many disciples, such as Khenpo Chöpa, Khenpo Gekpa, Khenpo Jikwang, and others, have manifested shrunken bodies, miraculous relics, and other auspicious signs after their death. A Han Chinese nun named Minghui attained accomplishment six months after studying and practicing the Great Perfection. There are also many disciples who were reborn in a pure realm such as the Blissful Pure Land, as evidenced by the auspicious signs at their death.

Other auspicious signs include the *sariras*, or miraculous pearls, that often fell from the sky during Jigme Phuntsok Rinpoche's teachings and Dharma assemblies. As such, it was as if the renowned ancient Nalanda in eastern India—the world's first Dharma institution—had reappeared on the earth. It is essential to visit Larung Gar in person to fully appreciate what is described here.

RESTORING A PURE SANGHA

Across the Tibetan region and elsewhere in China, Buddhism had suffered from years of calamities that brought chaos to the Buddhist sangha system. When conditions became favorable, the great Jigme Phuntsok Rinpoche began to focus on the propagation of the Vinaya Pitaka,[60] and assisted many monks in receiving the samanera and bhikkhu vows. He encouraged several larger sanghas to rally their forces, restore and rebuild their monasteries, clothe sangha members in monastic robes, and engage in extensive study and practice of the Dharma at the monastery.

In 1985, the year of the wood ox, Jigme Phuntsok Rinpoche bestowed the empowerment of Tertön Lerab Lingpa's *Complete Collected Works* on more than three thousand monastics. At that time, he realized that there were many problems within the monastic communities, such as breaking monastic and tantric vows, that made a major overhaul necessary. Thus, he immediately gathered abbots of Tibetan monasteries and renowned great masters to discuss the issue. They unanimously agreed with Jigme Phuntsok Rinpoche's proposal, believing that it was a matter of urgency to rectify the sanghas.

An open letter was then issued stating that a sangha member should study and practice the Dharma, uphold pure precepts, propagate the Buddha's teachings, and benefit living beings. The key message was that, except for a very few tantric masters[61] who are like "the bright moon surrounded by the myriads of stars," all the sangha members in the monastery must receive their ordination and uphold pure pratimoksha vows. In accordance with sutras and tantras, those who failed to uphold the pratimoksha vows and had broken their samaya vows would not be allowed to stay in the sangha. Sangha members should study and practice the Dharma seriously and turn their mind away from worldly concerns so that they would be qualified to accept offerings. This open letter would be like a miraculous panacea for the monasteries large and small, primarily in the eastern Tibetan region, reviving sanghas on the verge of destruction.

The rectification would encounter many unexpected oppositions and obstacles from monastics who had broken vows during the upheavals. Nevertheless, Jigme Phuntsok Rinpoche would prevail and eventually succeed in purifying the monastic communities. He once made this plaintive remark to a large group of monastics: "Before I started this rectification, I was respected and supported by all monastics and laypeople. After the rectification, many people hated me to the bone and slandered me for no reason. However, given the fact that Buddhism was like the setting sun, if no intervention had been introduced, Buddhism would have been doomed if left as it was. To carry on the legacy of the Buddha's teachings, I would rather give my life than retreat in the face of adversity. . . ."

All in all, the great Jigme Phuntsok Rinpoche would play an extremely important role in rectifying the sanghas in Tibetan monasteries and at large, so that nowadays many sangha members are able to uphold pure precepts and be well organized. This is also a very important milestone in the history of Buddhism.

The great Jigme Phuntsok Rinpoche with the sangha of the Larung Gar Five Sciences Buddhist Academy, 1992.

PURE ASPIRATION

After the open letter for rectifying the sangha was issued, its message rapidly spread all over the Tibetan region and caused an outcry among those who had failed to uphold their monastic vows or who had broken their samaya vows. They quickly gathered more opponents to the rectification and created obstacles to its progress. The pressure of this resistance was like a thousand-pound weight on the shoulders of Jigme Phuntsok Rinpoche. He later shared his thoughts from that time: "I can swear on my life, and testify to my lama and the Three Jewels with my pure motivation, that the rectification was solely driven by my sincere devotion to Buddhism, and I don't have the slightest selfish intention or a personal agenda. Why have I encountered so many difficulties and setbacks?" A faint shadow was cast over his heart.

In the evening of the eighteenth day of the third Tibetan month of 1985, in Jigme Phuntsok Rinpoche's luminous dream, his deity appeared to him amid colorful rays of light. The deity smiled warmly at him and said, "Good man, don't feel discouraged. You will surely be able to take up the important task of upholding Buddhism. The Buddha has clearly prophesied in *The Root Tantra of Manjushri* that your Dharma activities will be vast and grand." Then the deity disappeared.

The next day, Jigme Phuntsok Rinpoche called on Khenpo Tenzin Norbu and other disciples to look up the prophecy in the Tripitaka. Sure enough, it was clearly stated in *The Root Tantra of Manjushri* that a master whose name contains "Ah" would uphold the Buddha's teachings.[62]

On the fourth day of the sixth Tibetan month, Jigme Phuntsok Rinpoche made an enthusiastic announcement in front of over one thousand monastics: "Today, with the supreme bodhichitta, I vow to try my very best to guide all living beings in Jambudvipa[63] to liberation. If this is not possible, I will try my best to guide all living beings in this country to liberation. At the very least, I aspire to guide everyone in the Tibetan region onto the path of liberation."

The great Jigme Phuntsok Rinpoche in the Kalachakra empowerment ceremony at the Larung Gar Five Sciences Buddhist Academy, 1986.

DIRECT VISIONS OF
THE THREE MANJUSHRIS

Jigme Phuntsok Rinpoche established the Larung Gar Five Sciences Buddhist Academy as a nonsectarian center embracing the principles of the Rimé Movement.[64] His appreciation of the differences among lineages could be reflected in his direct visions of the Three Manjushris.

In the Tibetan region, there are three unanimously recognized emanations of Manjushri: the Sakya school's Sakya Pandita Kunga Gyaltsen (1182–1251), the Nyingma school's Longchenpa, and the Geluk school's Lama Tsongkhapa. Owing to his extraordinary power developed through Dharma practice, Jigme Phuntsok Rinpoche had a direct vision of each emanation and received transmissions, empowerments, and blessings from all of them.

SAKYA PANDITA

During his studies at Sershul, when he had just started studying Sakya Pandita Kunga Gyaltsen's *Treasury of Logic on Valid Cognition*, Jigme Phuntsok Rinpoche found it a bit difficult to understand certain specific terms of Buddhist logic. Therefore, he prayed to the lama and his deity wholeheartedly.

One evening, Sakya Pandita appeared in Jigme Phuntsok Rinpoche's luminous dream and transmitted to him the *Manjushri-Namasamgiti (Chanting the Names of Manjushri)* and granted him supreme blessings. When he excitedly awoke from the dream, he comprehended all the Sutrayana and Vajrayana teachings, and all his questions on Buddhist logic were resolved. During the dream,

Jigme Phuntsok Rinpoche had slept for two or three days, and when he woke up, he muttered, "I must have been sick."

LONGCHENPA

In the winter of the wood bird year of 1981, when Jigme Phuntsok Rinpoche was teaching the *Guhyagarbha Tantra* to a few thousand of his disciples, many auspicious signs appeared.

One day, Jigme Phuntsok Rinpoche was contemplating in his bedroom with his eyes closed, when suddenly, on opening his eyes, he saw Longchenpa and Yeshe Tsogyal descending from above him amid multicolored light. They bestowed on him the empowerment of the *Guhyagarbha Tantra*, then ascended into space and departed.

In great bliss, Jigme Phuntsok Rinpoche immediately wrote down the whole sadhana of the empowerment he had just received, which is now included in his collective works. This very sadhana is what Jigme Phuntsok Rinpoche used later to bestow the empowerment on his disciples at home and abroad.

TSONGKHAPA

On the twentieth day of the seventh Tibetan month in the fire tiger year of 1986, Jigme Phuntsok Rinpoche was sitting on his bed resting when suddenly a blinding white light flashed across his eyes and a great master appeared in front of him. The master was nobly dressed in a long-eared yellow pandita hat and kasaya. Jigme Phuntsok Rinpoche immediately recognized the master as Lama Tsongkhapa, so he went forth to pay homage.

Lama Tsongkhapa transmitted to him the *Three Principal Aspects of the Path*,[65] then said to him with a smile, "Now I dwell in the presence of Bodhisattva Maitreya, and my name is Jampal Nyingpo. If your disciples can memorize the *Three Principal Aspects of the Path* and engage in Sojong[66] practice, through the blessings of Dharmata—or the true nature of reality—they will surely be reborn in the Tushita Heaven to enjoy the Dharma bliss. In the future when I attain Buddhahood as Tathagata Simhanada,[67] they will become my first disciples." After saying this, Lama Tsongkhapa turned into light and disappeared.

Jigme Phuntsok Rinpoche recounted this experience to his disciples. Later, many Geluk *geshes*[68] and monks from nearby counties, such as Dawu and Draggo, came to request transmission of the *Three Principal Aspects of the Path*. Following Tsongkhapa's advice, more and more people started to memorize this text and engage in Sojong practice.

Since the great Jigme Phuntsok Rinpoche had direct visions of lineage holders from several traditions of Tibetan Buddhism, he helped foster a harmonious relationship among the major schools such as Geluk, Sakya, and Nyingma in Tibetan Buddhism.

The Power of Divine Vision

As previously mentioned, Jigme Phuntsok Rinpoche began to exhibit supernatural abilities at the young age of five or six. Now, let's delve into a few stories showcasing his divine vision as an adult.

Dzilo and the Snake

There were many poisonous snakes in the Tibetan forests, so it was common for people to die from snakebites. But, with an enlightened master's foresight, the victim of a fatal snakebite could be spared.

When Jigme Phuntsok Rinpoche was living in a place called Yarchen, an old woman named Dzilo from Nubzur village often herded her horses on a nearby hillside. One day around noon, she paid a visit to Jigme Phuntsok Rinpoche when he was having lunch with his family. They warmly welcomed her and shared their meal.

While eating, Jigme Phuntsok Rinpoche chatted with her.

"Do you have deer musk at home?"

"Yes, I do. It's wrapped in a leather bag," she answered, without thinking too much.

"Do you know how to avoid venom poisoning after a snakebite on the foot?"

Dzilo seemed unconcerned, answering, "No, I don't."

"If you are bitten by a venomous snake, you must soak the deer musk in water for a while, then apply it to the bite. This way, you can detoxify the poison." After lunch, as Dzilo prepared to leave, Jigme Phuntsok Rinpoche reminded her several more times how to use deer musk, which she acknowledged rather indifferently.

Dzilo bid farewell and headed back home with her horses.

When she arrived at a place called Yachung, she sat down to take a break and a venomous snake bit her. Enduring the intense pain, she hurried home, but nobody was there. She thought to herself, "What should I do? Once the poison starts to spread, there is no way to save my life." She suddenly remembered Jigme Phuntsok Rinpoche's advice and immediately took out the deer musk and applied it to her wound as instructed. As a result, she was saved from death. From then on, Dzilo generated great faith in Jigme Phuntsok Rinpoche and would tell whomever she encountered about his great qualities.

KHENPO CHÖPA'S HOUSE

There was a khenpo named Chöpa, who was brought up only by his mother. Although Chöpa and his mother were not wealthy, they lived a decent life and owned a few treasures passed down from their ancestors. When he grew up, Chöpa became an ordained monk and received the khenpo degree under Jigme Phuntsok Rinpoche's guidance.

Once, Chöpa spent an entire day receiving a practice guidance that he requested from Jigme Phuntsok Rinpoche. At noon that day, Jigme Phuntsok Rinpoche invited Chöpa for lunch. They were joyfully chatting while eating yogurt and tsampa balls when Jigme Phuntsok Rinpoche suddenly stopped and said, "Oh no! Something is wrong at your home!"

He handed Khenpo Chöpa a phurba, telling him, "Go outside immediately, point the dagger toward your home, and recite aloud the Vajrakilaya mantra."[69]

Khenpo Chöpa was a bit anxious. He quickly ran out and started reciting the mantra loudly in the direction of his home. At the same time, Jigme Phuntsok Rinpoche started reciting the Vajrakilaya mantra earnestly and loudly: OM BANZER GELE GELAYA HUNG PHAD.

After a while, Jigme Phuntsok Rinpoche stopped and said to Khenpo Chöpa, who was outside, "Everything's alright now."

Khenpo Chöpa came in and asked, "What just happened at my home?"

"Nothing! Everything is fine now!" Jigme Phuntsok Rinpoche replied.

After lunch, Khenpo Chöpa hurried back home to find out what had taken place. His mother had left home to herd their cattle in the mountains, leaving the house unattended. A thief sneaked in, searched for their valuables, and put them all in a bag. As he was about to leave, suddenly his body started to tremble all over. He was so frightened that he dropped the bag and fled.

The great Jigme Phuntsok Rinpoche smiles at disciples from his cabin at the Larung Gar Five Sciences Buddhist Academy in the mid-1990s.

The great Jigme Phuntsok Rinpoche hosting a Dharma assembly in front of the Grand Dharma Hall at the Larung Gar Five Sciences Buddhist Academy, 1992.

THE DEPENDENT ARISING[70] OF
HIS DHARMA ACTIVITIES

Unlike ordinary people who often act out of impulse, great masters will not only deliberate in advance but also carefully observe the dependent arising of anything they plan to do.

In 1986, at the invitation of renowned monasteries in the Dokham region, Jigme Phuntsok Rinpoche visited them and went on pilgrimages to sacred mountains with some of his disciples. During his stay at Nenang Monastery, the sangha there not only provided Jigme Phuntsok Rinpoche the best accommodations and provisions but also offered numerous highly valuable objects and gifts as a token of veneration.

Jigme Phuntsok Rinpoche gathered the sangha and said, "I don't really need these offerings. Among them, I'll only accept two objects. One is a cushion, and the other is a bridle. Today, I want to observe the dependent arising. Let us recite the mantra of dependent arising in the presence of the Three Jewels, and then we'll see which of these two objects will be chosen. If the cushion is chosen, it means I will settle down in one place to propagate the Dharma; if the bridle is chosen, it means I will travel widely to benefit sentient beings with the Dharma."

The sangha gathered and started reciting the mantra before the representations of the Three Jewels, which have extremely strong blessing power. In the end, the decision landed on the bridle through drawing lots. With a smile, Jigme Phuntsok Rinpoche picked up the bridle and said, "In that case, from now on I will start traveling for the sake of propagating the Dharma and benefiting sentient beings. Next year, I will make a pilgrimage to Mount Wutai, and after that, I will travel to other countries one by one."

Later, they arrived at the sacred mountain Bazhab Drakkar, where Jigme Phuntsok Rinpoche obtained a rare treasure called Cloud Gem. Here is how the treasure was obtained:

One day, while giving a teaching to several thousand monastics and laypeople, Jigme Phuntsok Rinpoche told everyone, "There may be a very special stone in this place. Whoever finds it, please give it to me. This stone is of no use to you, but if I have it, it will be of great help to my Dharma activities. This stone remains damp whether the temperature is hot or cold, and it occasionally radiates a dazzling black light."

A few days later, when Jigme Phuntsok Rinpoche was staying at the sacred mountain Belo Ritro, a herdsman brought the stone to him. Jigme Phuntsok Rinpoche was delighted and said, "The dependent arising of my future Dharma activities relies upon this treasure." He then offered the herdsman a white *khata*, or traditional ceremonial scarf. But, when Jigme Phuntsok Rinpoche held the stone in his hand and checked it carefully, he found that it was stained and had lost its luster.

The herdsman then explained the history of the stone: One day, a loud thundering sound came from the sky. The herdsman went out and noticed that a magnificent oval-shaped stone had fallen near his tent. He picked it up and put it in the tent. In the family, there was an old man who smoked snuff. The old man often used this stone to grind his shag tobacco. Eventually the stone became so tainted that it completely lost its original luster.

In no time, Jigme Phuntsok Rinpoche conducted a smoke purification ritual, then washed the stone repeatedly. He recited Buddhist texts and mantras to bless and reconsecrate the stone. Gradually, the Cloud Gem regained its original purity and luster. This special stone has helped create very auspicious dependent arising for Jigme Phuntsok Rinpoche's Dharma activities.

THE DISCOVERY OF ANCIENT CAVES

One year in the mid-1980s, the great Jigme Phuntsok Rinpoche led many disciples on a pilgrimage to the sacred Mount Bané. On the seventeenth day of the first Tibetan month of that year, when the upper rim of the sun appeared on the horizon in the morning, Jigme Phuntsok Rinpoche entered the state of meditative absorption, and in his vision many dakini scripts appeared. He immediately told his attendant, "Please bring a pen and paper!" Then he had someone write down the following lines:

> To the right of this place in the southeast direction,
> One-third the way up a red heart jewel,
> In the middle of the mirrorlike plain and amidst trees,
> There are handprints, writings, stupas, and tsok offerings.
> Girls born in the tiger year may present khatas and wine,
> And if the timing is not missed, the objects can be found.

Then Jigme Phuntsok Rinpoche gathered ten girls and ten boys who were born in the year of tiger, and said to them, "Now please head southeast to search for a cave. Its position is about one-third the way up a big heart-shaped rock. The rock is situated in the middle of a grassy meadow as flat as a mirror, and the surroundings and the entrance of the cave are concealed by many trees."

After that, with his entourage, Jigme Phuntsok Rinpoche went to a nearby cave where Padmasambhava had meditated. He consecrated the cave by chanting prayers, causing nectar to flow naturally. Those who stayed outside of the cave could clearly hear wonderful sounds and smell fragrant aromas coming from within. Then they made the Manjushri tsok offerings.

At that time, the children who were sent to search for the meditation cave returned and reported on their searching process and the approximate location of a cave. Jigme Phuntsok Rinpoche was very pleased, and said with a smile, "The omen is very auspicious and perfect." He called forth several disciples and told them, "Please go there and enter another cave—the secret dakini cave—on the right side of the mountain. Make sure to check carefully to see whether you can find any naturally manifested Buddha statues, handprints of dakinis, Buddhist scriptures, stupas, and dakinis' tsok offering-substances." It turned out that all those objects were discovered one by one. In this way, Vimalamitra's meditation cave and the dakinis' secret cave were discovered.

Jigme Phuntsok Rinpoche was not the first one searching for the two caves. Many great masters had gone through various hardships in search of these two mysterious ancient caves that were known according to past prophecies, but their efforts were to no avail because the causes and conditions were not yet ready for the caves to be found. This time, Jigme Phuntsok Rinpoche successfully found these two hidden caves according to the terma revealed by Tertön Matiratna.

Jigme Phuntsok Rinpoche remarked, "Meditating in these caves can bring practitioners exceptionally powerful blessings. Specifically, practicing in Vimalamitra's cave can help eliminate mind-wandering, and by meditating in the cave for seven days a practitioner can be taken directly under the care of Vimalamitra and receive a hundred instructions on meditation. In the dakinis' secret cave, if a practitioner has mastered the practices of the generation stage and the completion stage, by making tsok offerings one hundred thousand times they are certain to go to a pure realm without leaving the material body behind."

Extraordinary Signs of Accomplishment

In addition to his vast Dharma activities, Jigme Phuntsok Rinpoche displayed extraordinary signs of his spiritual accomplishment to his fortunate followers.

Recognized as a Mahasiddha

The *mahasiddhas*, or fully perfected ones who have attained all the inner realizations, can have multiple emanations at the same time in order to benefit living beings. According to the aforementioned prophecy by Tertön Pawo Chöying Dorjé, when Jigme Phuntsok Rinpoche was Lerab Lingpa in his previous life, he also manifested as the great mahasiddha of Dawu, Kunzang Chödrak (1823–1905).

Kunzang Chödrak was a highly achieved master, renowned for his profound wisdom and ultimate realization. This is reflected in his words spoken just before he passed into parinirvana. At that time, his attendant Ahwa asked him with sorrow, "Dear lama, after your passing, where should we go to look for the child of your reincarnation? Please also kindly tell us what this Dharma center will continue to be?"

Kunzang Chödrak smiled and said, "Regarding my reincarnation, you don't have to exhaust yourselves searching everywhere. In the future, someone who can recite *Chanting the Names of Manjushri* at will is going to come here and rebuild this center. He is my reincarnation." Afterward, while rubbing his alms bowl, Kunzang Chödrak talked about the merits of upholding precepts, and eventually entered parinirvana peacefully.

After discovering the two secret caves, the great Jigme Phun-tsok Rinpoche and his entourage made a pilgrimage to the sacred Mount Gobo Lhatse. At that time, those eminent masters from Minyak identified with certainty that Jigme Phuntsok Rinpoche was the reincarnation of Kunzang Chödrak, based on evidence such as Tertön Pawo Chöying Dorjé's prophecy and the fact that Jigme Phuntsok Rinpoche could recite *Chanting the Names of Manjushri* at will.

Jigme Phuntsok Rinpoche established an affiliated center there and expounded teachings such as *Chanting the Names of Manjushri* and *The Way of the Bodhisattva* to many Buddhist believers. He also taught *Bardo Thodol*, or *The Tibetan Book of the Dead*, to Buddhists who were suitable recipients of the tantric teaching.

EXTRAORDINARY DEEDS

To ordinary people, rocks are so hard that it is impossible to leave a hand imprint on them or to directly take something out of them. However, it is not unusual for mahasiddhas with perfect inner realization to do so. They possess the ability to easily transform the four primary elements[71] from one form to another, let alone to leave an imprint on a rock. With the power of their past great aspirations, their present meditative absorption, and the right causes and conditions, it is easy for them to perform such actions.

In 1986, on the auspicious day of Buddha Shakyamuni's descent from heaven,[72] the summit of Mount Gobo Lhatse was crammed with Buddhist devotees. Jigme Phuntsok Rinpoche sat for a brief meditative session next to a large rock, after which he took a statue of Buddha Shakyamuni out of the rock. The crowd was awestruck by what they witnessed. This statue was entrusted by Padmasam-bhava to dharmapalas, who were asked to hand it over to the ema-nation of Nanam Dorjé Dudjom in the future. After revealing this Buddha statue, Jigme Phuntsok Rinpoche immediately granted blessings to the crowd with it. Later, he stepped on a giant rock and left a one-inch-deep footprint.

SPONTANEOUS MANIFESTATIONS

In the Tibetan region, one can often find the mani mantra, or the mantra of Avalokiteshvara—OM MANI PADME HUNG—carved on the rock walls of mountains. There are also numerous mani piles consisting of stones into which the mantra has been meticulously inscribed. Nevertheless, it is rare to see a mani mantra that has spontaneously appeared on rocks through a great master's realization power from their inner yoga practice.

When the great Jigme Phuntsok Rinpoche was practicing the Red Avalokiteshvara and reciting the mani mantra at Mount Gobo Lhatse, the mantra spontaneously appeared on many of the rocks in that area, which amazed everyone. Sometimes, while onlookers were watching, a clearly visible red-colored Avalokiteshvara mantra would appear on rocks. A few decades have passed since then, but the mantras on the rocks are still very noticeable.

There are many sacred mountains full of blessing power in the Land of Snows, and Mount Mudo is one of them. Many great masters attained extraordinary accomplishments at Mount Mudo. It is also one of the sacred mountains specially blessed by Padmasambhava. Thus, many practitioners consider Mount Mudo a great place for practice. Once, Jigme Phuntsok Rinpoche took his disciples there on pilgrimage and performed rituals of consecration and purification at the foot of the mountain. Then, two stupas in the shape of the Bodhi Pagoda, which symbolizes the Buddha's attainment of enlightenment, miraculously appeared in the mountain from nowhere. Many auspicious signs had appeared there in the past, so the locals were no longer easily surprised. However, it was the first time they witnessed the miraculous scene of two stupas spontaneously rising from the ground.

POURING THE NECTAR OF DHARMA

In the same year, the great Jigme Phuntsok Rinpoche visited seventy-two monasteries of the Geluk, Nyingma, Sakya, and

Kagyu lineages primarily in the Tibetan regions of Dawu, Draggo, Dartsedo, and Garze. He made pilgrimages to the five sacred mountains that represent Padmasambhava's body, speech, mind, qualities, and activities. Jigme Phuntsok Rinpoche instructed the sanghas of the monasteries, saying, "All of you Buddhist practitioners should focus on hearing, contemplating, and meditating. If you don't study and practice the Dharma, that is truly shameful. As monks, you shouldn't blindly follow the footsteps of deluded worldly beings living in this degenerate era. Instead, you should apply the true Dharma to tame your minds."

During the trip, Jigme Phuntsok Rinpoche poured the nectar of Dharma over the seventy-two monasteries and many other small and large Buddhist institutions, and reconsecrated and purified the many sacred mountains that were heavily contaminated by the negative energy from the many years of turmoil. Furthermore, he urged many laypeople to adopt the ten virtuous actions and give up wrongdoings such as stealing. He also suggested that each layperson recite the Manjushri mantra at least one hundred million times. As a result, ever since then people in the Kham region are more likely to engage in positive actions.

THE START OF HIS DHARMA ACTIVITIES IN THE HAN AREA OF CHINA

In 1986, Jigme Phuntsok Rinpoche made a heartfelt commitment to bring the nourishing nectar of the Dharma to the Han Chinese people. Because the Han area of China is considered the earthly abode of Manjushri, he decided to begin with a pilgrimage to Mount Wutai—the sacred mountain of Manjushri.

The dependent arising of this pilgrimage was demonstrated to over six thousand attendees during a morning when Jigme Phuntsok Rinpoche was bestowing the empowerment of the *Illusory Net of Manjushri*. While he was reciting the sadhana to invoke deities, his whole body suddenly levitated from the throne and hovered in the air for a short time, then he slowly descended back to his throne. He stayed in the state of meditative absorption for a long time, then said to everyone calmly, "Just now, Manjushri and Vimalamitra from Mount Wutai appeared in my inner visionary manifestation and invoked us for a visit. From now on, I will establish connections with people in the Han area and guide them on the path of liberation. In the future, there may be many Han disciples coming to study and practice the Dharma at our Buddhist academy. They will also spread the Sutrayana and Vajrayana teachings all over the world."

The omen about their pilgrimage to Mount Wutai also emerged clearly in the same year during Jigme Phuntsok Rinpoche's pilgrimage to a sacred mountain. When visiting Mount Sotok, he walked into the Yamantaka cave and said to his disciples, "This sacred mountain of Manjushri is full of blessing power. Next year we are going to make a pilgrimage to Mount Wutai, so now we must establish an auspicious dependent arising. I shall first make a Manjushri tsok offering, so please go outside." He then meditated in the cave alone.

To invoke Dharmapala Yamantaka during the tsok offering, Jigme Phuntsok Rinpoche, through meditation, came to know that a twelve-year-old girl was needed for the ritual, but there was only an eleven-year-old girl present. After the tsok offering, Jigme Phuntsok Rinpoche came out of the cave and started circumambulating the sacred mountain. Then a monk dressed in a yellow robe walked toward Jigme Phuntsok Rinpoche and said to him with a smile, "I am very happy that you and your entourage are going on a pilgrimage to Mount Wutai next year. Here I have a copy of *The Annals of Mount Wutai*." He handed the book to Jigme Phuntsok Rinpoche and soon disappeared without a trace.

Jigme Phuntsok Rinpoche opened the book and discovered that it was written in Tibetan. But, strangely enough, there were handwritten notes in ancient Chinese on the edge of the book pages. Jigme Phuntsok Rinpoche said, "This is a terma personally delivered by a dharmapala. Because we didn't find a twelve-year-old girl for the tsok offering, the omen is slightly inauspicious, so this book might not be complete." The disciples examined the book closely and noticed that indeed one page was missing.

The Direct Vision of Manjushri

In order to propagate the Dharma in the Han area of China, on the sixth day of the fourth Tibetan month in 1987, the great Jigme Phuntsok Rinpoche set out on the pilgrimage to Mount Wutai with his entourage. On the departure day, the Larung Gar Five Sciences Buddhist Academy was unlike before: the sangha members got up very early and made their final preparations before setting out on the journey. The sun shone in the cloudless blue sky and seemed brighter than usual.

There were more than ten thousand Tibetans following Jigme Phuntsok Rinpoche on the pilgrimage. What a spectacular group! Some of them left earlier by truck, heading for Mount Wutai by the route passing Kumbum Monastery.[73] Jigme Phuntsok Rinpoche and several of his disciples first visited Chengdu, where they made a pilgrimage to the famous sacred sites including Mount Emei[74] and Leshan.[75] Afterward, they flew to Beijing. They continued to travel until they arrived at Mount Wutai, located at the northeast of the city of Taiyuan, Shanxi Province. It was spring at that time, and Mount Wutai was adorned with green trees and pleasant breezes. Tibetan pilgrims from Sichuan, Qinghai, Tibet, and other provinces began to pour in, and monks in red monastic robes almost filled the entire Mount Wutai, adding unprecedented charm to this renowned sacred site.

The Tibetan pilgrims displayed great adaptability at Mount Wutai, despite being unfamiliar with the place. Many of them had to sleep outdoors but were nevertheless very much at ease. Their carefree manner was truly commendable.

Many Buddhist devotees from the Han area of China were also attracted to Mount Wutai. The dependent conditions were favorable, and auspicious signs could be witnessed everywhere. To the Mongolian and Han Chinese Buddhists who joined the pilgrimage, the great Jigme Phuntsok Rinpoche transmitted teachings such as *The Concise Treatise on the Stages of the Path to Enlightenment, Thirty-Seven Practices of the Bodhisattvas,* and other teachings. In front of Buddha Shakyamuni's reliquary stupa, in accordance with the aspiration of benefiting sentient beings, Jigme Phuntsok Rinpoche recited *The King of Aspiration Prayers: Samantabhadra's "Aspiration to Good Actions"* with his entourage and also made the aspiration that all beings who had established a connection with him would take rebirth in the Blissful Pure Land.

In order to widely propagate the Nyingma teachings, Jigme Phuntsok Rinpoche built statues of Padmasambhava in more than fifty temples at Mount Wutai. Furthermore, he renovated the Manjushri Hall, the Tsongkhapa Hall, and others. From that point onward, Jigme Phuntsok Rinpoche began accepting non-Tibetan disciples, primarily those of Han Chinese descent.

The statue of Guru Rinpoche Padmasambhava at the sacred Mount Wutai that the great Jigme Phuntsok Rinpoche built and consecrated in 1987.

The great Jigme Phuntsok Rinpoche at Mount Wutai, 1987.

Since his arrival at Mount Wutai, Jigme Phuntsok Rinpoche had been staying at a place called the Bodhisattva Summit. One day, after giving a teaching to a few thousand Buddhist devotees, he moved to the Sudhana Cave in the afternoon without giving any prior notice. Shortly after his arrival at the cave, seven children appeared out of nowhere. They listened to Jigme Phuntsok Rinpoche's teaching respectfully, then vanished without a trace. Then Jigme Phuntsok Rinpoche went into a strictly solitary retreat. On the twenty-ninth day of the fourth Tibetan month, Manjushri—the wisdom embodiment of all buddhas of the past, present, and future—appeared vividly in his pure vision. Manjushri was golden in color, wearing a ritual five-buddha crown on his head; he had one face and two arms, with his left hand holding a Buddhist scripture and his right hand holding a sword up high; and he was sitting in the vajra posture, adorned with the ornaments of the

Seven children listen to the great Jigme Phuntsok Rinpoche's teaching near the Sudhana Cave at Mount Wutai, 1987.

The great Jigme Phuntsok Rinpoche, Mount Wutai, 1987.

sambhogakaya,[76] and staying in a peaceful form. Jigme Phuntsok Rinpoche was overwhelmed with joy, and his faith and devotion grew even stronger. Right away, he started to sing a vajra song:

> I am just like a helpless child eagerly await the sight of my mother.
> I have been searching for you day and night with fervent devotion,
> But before this moment, I had no idea at all where you were.
> This time, with tens of thousands of my disciples,
> I have traveled thousands of miles,
> Gone through many hardships,
> And arrived here from the Tibetan region,
> All because I wanted to find you . . .

Before Manjushri, Jigme Phuntsok Rinpoche made a vow: "Life after life I shall liberate all the suffering beings who are trapped in samsara. I shall help them be freed from the shackles of karma, attain the unsurpassable bliss, and enter the ultimate Dharmadhatu." During this period, he also composed several works illuminating the supreme pith instructions, such as *Heartfelt Advice from the Essential Heart*, which arose spontaneously from the wisdom of his pristine awareness.

After that, Jigme Phuntsok Rinpoche spent another fourteen days doing a solitary retreat in the Narayana Cave, where, according to the *Flower Garland Sutra*, or the *Avatamsaka Sutra*, Manjushri resides. Jigme Phuntsok Rinpoche recalled, "During the whole retreat, I had been resting in the state of luminosity day and night." Blessed by Manjushri's wisdom, he composed *The Great Perfection of the Peaceful Manjushri: Placing Buddhahood within Reach* and other extraordinary texts. Meanwhile, King Gesar and other dharmapalas vowed to do their utmost to protect and help Jigme Phuntsok Rinpoche's Dharma activities.

In accordance with their own levels of connection with Manjushri, some of his disciples had direct visions of Manjushri's

The great Jigme Phuntsok Rinpoche giving a teaching at
Mount Wutai, 1987.

mudra,[77] mantra, sword, and other signs. Essentially, what they
saw in their direct visions were the numerous signs of Manjushri's
rupakaya, or form body, as described in *The Annals of Mount
Wutai*. What is more amazing is that some disciples with superior
faculties fully realized the ultimate Manjushri—the true nature of
their own mind.

ACCEPTING HAN CHINESE DISCIPLES

Since he was a child, Jigme Phuntsok Rinpoche had generated indescribable faith in Manjushri and had an intense desire to personally visit Mount Wutai, the abode of Manjushri. Prior to the pilgrimage in 1987, he had already visited Mount Wutai three times in his illusory body through the practice of luminous dreaming.

One day, when he was in the Sudhana Cave during the pilgrimage, the great Jigme Phuntsok Rinpoche told his disciples, "I have visited this sacred place three times in my dreams. In one of the dreams, I found a broken stone statue of Manjushri under a tree near a temple at the middle peak.[78] Now would you please go there and look for the statue?" His disciples immediately set out for the middle peak, and indeed found the stone statue of Manjushri under the tree. The statue was brought back to the Larung Gar Five Sciences Buddhist Academy in Sertar and is now placed on the shrine of the Manjushri Hall on Mount Garuda.

During over a hundred unforgettable days at Mount Wutai, Jigme Phuntsok Rinpoche transmitted Longchenpa's *Seven Treasuries* and many other Sutrayana and Vajrayana teachings to Tibetan and Chinese monks, nuns, and laypeople. To benefit future living beings, Jigme Phuntsok Rinpoche also entrusted dharmapalas with many termas, so that they are concealed in various ways in that sacred place. In the future, when the right causes and conditions come together, the termas will be revealed by a destined tertön and bring benefit to innumerable beings in the Han area of China.

When Jigme Phuntsok Rinpoche was about to set off on his journey back to Larung Gar, the Buddhist devotees from the Han area pleaded with him not to leave. They said, "Even if you must return to the Tibetan region now, please return to Mount Wutai as soon as possible and stay here for a long time."

Jigme Phuntsok Rinpoche said to them affectionately:

In the spring when flowers bloomed,
I came to Mount Wutai with the cuckoo birds.
The birds sang you beautiful songs,
While I taught you the precious Dharma,
And we enjoyed the bliss of Dharma together.

Now, changing foliage and crisp winds signal that autumn
    has arrived.
The cuckoo birds are going back to the Mongolian area,
And I will return to the Land of Snows.
What has been gathered will be dispersed,
And what is born will surely die—
This is the law of nature that no one can change.

Although you haven't asked the cuckoo birds,
They will nevertheless come here and sing for you again next
    year.
Despite that you have earnestly pleaded with me to return,
I may not have the opportunity to revisit here, as I am old
    and frail.

I hope you will adopt positive actions and abandon negative
    ones,
And that you practice the true Dharma wholeheartedly.
If we don't have the chance to meet again in this life,
We will surely reunite in the Blissful Pure Land in the near
    future.

On an early misty morning, Jigme Phuntsok Rinpoche waved goodbye to Mount Wutai and the crowd of Han Chinese, which was reluctant to part from him. A group of Han Chinese monks, clad in the yellow monastic robes of Chinese Buddhism, followed him back to Larung Gar and started their lifelong journey of studying and practicing Tibetan Buddhism. The arrival of this Han Chinese sangha at a Tibetan Dharma center was a milestone in the history of Tibetan Buddhism.

From then on, Han Chinese monastics from all corners of the country and even across the world have been continuously turning up at the Larung Valley, where they engage in systematic study and practice of the Dharma. Initially few in number, the Han Chinese sangha has grown into a large community with many learned monastics.

TRULY A MAGNIFICENT FEAT

One of Jigme Phuntsok Rinpoche's significant Dharma achievements is the establishment of a large-scale female sangha at Larung Gar, made up of both Tibetans and Han Chinese. This undertaking was unprecedented in the history of Tibetan Buddhism. Ever since Buddhism was introduced into the Tibetan region from India in the seventh century, the Land of Snows has been recognized as a central place in terms of the Dharma, and faith in the Three Jewels has penetrated every corner of Tibetan people's lives. However, throughout Tibetan history, there have been very few female monastics, in contrast to the large male monastic community.

In addition to specific historical traditions, this lack of nuns can be attributed to the Buddha's teachings in some sutras. Specifically, in some of the Buddha's teachings it is said that women have more mental afflictions and other faults than men; therefore, if a Dharma master hasn't developed sufficient qualities before taking female monastics into the sangha, doing so will create obstacles for the master's Dharma activities. For this reason, it was very rare to find a master who widely accepted nuns into the sangha.

Over a hundred years ago, Lama Drakkar Lobzang Palden (1866–1929), from Draggo county in Garze, included more than one hundred nuns in his sangha—a rare occurrence in history. In 1988, Jigme Phuntsok Rinpoche publicly stated, "Out of his compassion, our great teacher Buddha Shakyamuni allowed females to have the same opportunity as males to receive ordination. However, due to various reasons, there has never been a large-scale sangha of nuns in the Tibetan region. In order to free women from their worldly preoccupations so that they can pursue the Dharma with their precious human lives, from now on I will start to widely accept female monastics and establish a sangha of nuns."

As soon as these vajra words were spoken, a few dozen Tibetan women renounced their worldly life and came to Larung Gar to study and practice the Dharma with Jigme Phuntsok Rinpoche. Within a few years, the number of nuns had rapidly grown to several thousand, significantly surpassing that of the male monks. Also unprecedented in Tibetan history, Jigme Phuntsok Rinpoche accepted many ethnically Han Chinese women as nuns. The male sangha members couldn't help but be amazed by the remarkable number of female sangha members.

The female sangha members at Larung Gar stood out as learned Buddhist practitioners and scholars. Every year, Jigme Phuntsok Rinpoche would accord the highest degree of study—*khenmo*—to several well-versed nuns, who would then give Dharma teachings elsewhere across the country. As such, nowadays many nuns who trained at Larung Gar are playing crucial roles in upholding the victory banner of the Dharma.

Acknowledging the significant size of the female sangha at Larung Gar in 1999, a journalist wrote in his article "Sanskrit Chants in the Clouds"[79]:

> I have been to Drepung Monastery in Tibet, Kumbum Monastery in Qinghai, and Labrang Monastery in Gansu. . . . They are all well-known for their grand architectures and large number of sangha members. Nevertheless, they are outshined when compared to the Larung Gar Five Sciences Buddhist Academy in Sertar, which has a population of over seven thousand sangha members, monks and nuns included. The size of the Larung sangha is a world record . . .
>
> Although this Buddhist Academy at Larung Gar is not a nunnery per se, given the number of nuns here, I couldn't find anywhere else that is comparable. The size

The Larung Gar nuns with Jetsünma Muntso Rinpoche, the niece of the great Jigme Phuntsok Rinpoche, near the Mandala Stupa at the Larung Gar Five Sciences Buddhist Academy, 1998.

of the nun's community here can be counted as another world record...

This Academy of Tibetan Buddhism, which was established on the roof of the world at an altitude of over 4,000 meters, has been developing so fast. This can also be considered a world record.

MEETING WITH THE
TENTH PANCHEN LAMA

The successive Panchen Lamas are acknowledged as the emanation of Buddha Amitabha. To Tibetans, the Panchen Lama is the embodiment of the Buddha's compassion and wisdom and is honored as the second highest spiritual leader.

In the summer of 1986, during his tour to the Tibetan region, the Tenth Panchen Lama Chökyi Gyaltsen (1938–1989) came to Sertar to meet with Jigme Phuntsok Rinpoche. During the meeting, the Tenth Panchen Lama greatly praised Jigme Phuntsok Rinpoche's remarkable feat of establishing a Buddhist academy.

In the spring of 1987, when Jigme Phuntsok Rinpoche was on his way to Mount Wutai for a pilgrimage with his disciples and followers, he stopped by Beijing and met with the Tenth Panchen Lama again. Both great masters were very happy to see each other, and they had pleasant conversations together. The Tenth Panchen Lama highly praised Jigme Phuntsok Rinpoche's contribution in reviving Buddhism, upholding the Dharma, and rectifying sanghas. He also calligraphed the academy's name, "The Larung Temple and Five Sciences Buddhist Academy in Sertar," in Tibetan upon Jigme Phuntsok Rinpoche's request. The two great masters visited the Buddha's Tooth Relic Stupa located at the Lingguang Temple in Beijing and held a grand consecration ceremony, during which all attendees recited auspicious prayers for the prosperity of Buddhism and the vast propagation of Dharma.

In 1988, the Tenth Panchen Lama sent a personal letter to invite Jigme Phuntsok Rinpoche for another visit to Beijing to give teachings at the High-Level Tibetan Buddhism College of China, which the Tenth Panchen Lama founded in 1987. Jigme Phuntsok Rinpoche gladly accepted the invitation. During his over two-month stay, Jigme Phuntsok Rinpoche gave Dharma teachings, including Mipham Rinpoche's *Beacon of Certainty*, to Buddhist masters from Nyingma, Geluk, Sakya, and other schools. He also bestowed profound empowerments, imparted practical guidance, and gave pith instructions. The Tenth Panchen Lama expressed his appreciation and admiration again and again, praising Jigme Phuntsok Rinpoche for his extraordinary wisdom.

Later, the Tenth Panchen Lama invited Jigme Phuntsok Rinpoche to go with him to the renowned Tashi Lhunpo Monastery.[80] On their arrival, the two masters were warmly welcomed by the sangha members. There, they presided over the grand consecration ceremony for the stupas of the fifth to the ninth Panchen Lamas. During his stay, Jigme Phuntsok Rinpoche also gave a talk about how the Tibetan Buddhist schools and lineages don't contradict each other on the ultimate views, which he supported with scriptural evidence and logical reasoning. The talk garnered high praise from eminent masters of different lineages.

The great Jigme Phuntsok Rinpoche with the Tenth Panchen Lama, Beijing, 1987.

Padmasambhava in His Pure Vision

Samye Monastery was the first Buddhist monastery in Tibetan history and the place that hosted the first group of Tibetan monastics. It is a sacred place blessed by Padmasambhava and many other vidyadharas who all propagated Vajrayana teachings there.

When Jigme Phuntsok Rinpoche visited Lhasa in 1989, the abbot of Samye Monastery cordially invited him to give teachings there. On Jigme Phuntsok Rinpoche's arrival, the sangha was putting up a tall victory banner symbolizing the proliferation of Dharma in the main hall. Given this auspicious sign, Jigme Phuntsok Rinpoche composed a prayer on the spot in praise of victory banners.

While giving his teaching, Jigme Phuntsok Rinpoche vividly recalled the scenes from his past life when all twenty-five main disciples of Padmasambhava—including himself (as Nanam Dorjé Dudjom), King Trisong Detsen, and others—received the innermost secret heart-essence instructions from Padmasambhava at Samye. In utmost devotion he prayed to Padmasambhava, saying, "Back then, in this place, you transmitted profound teachings to your disciples, and you were so loving and kind to Khandro Yeshe Tsogyel, myself Nanam Dorjé Dudjom, and other disciples. But now, you are in the pure realm, and I am in this turbid world, guiding those who are resistant and difficult to lead. Please bless me and all sentient beings."

Jigme Phuntsok Rinpoche continued his teaching in a sentimental tone, "All conditioned things are impermanent. Back then, when Guru Rinpoche transmitted the tantric teachings to us, Samye Monastery was glorious and majestic, but now everything has changed." He recalled the tantric teachings that Padmasambhava had given upon Nanam Dorjé Dudjom's request. Then, Jigme Phuntsok Rinpoche rested in his pure awareness and spontaneously composed a profound tantric text out of his pristine wisdom. He then told his disciples, "If you can recite this tantric text often, you will definitely realize the Great Perfection." In fact, this extraordinary Samye composition summarizes the pith instructions given in Longchenpa's *Treasury of Word and Meaning* and is now compiled in Jigme Phuntsok Rinpoche's collective works. In addition, he composed an aspirational prayer here, wishing for the prosperity of teachings from all lineages and schools.

Later, on the way to the Chimpuk Hermitage near Samye, Jigme Phuntsok Rinpoche encountered a group of Tibetan herders who were chanting aloud the mantra of Padmasambhava, OM AH HUM VAJRA GURU PADMA SIDDHI HUM, which echoed through the valley. Owing to this, in his natural state of realization Jigme Phuntsok Rinpoche had a direct vision of Padmasambhava and his enlightened assembly. He passionately sang the following vajra song:

Please listen, dear fortunate ones!
The yogi's perception that samsara and nirvana are equal
Is like the immediate presence of Padmasambhava and his
    enlightened assembly—
There is no need to search for other pure lands.
My heart center is the Palace of Copper-Colored Mountain.
I see the faces of awareness holders and dakinis directly.
Today, I am so fortunate to arrive here at this place.
Everything is pure and pristine, full of enlightened art,
    letters, and sacred footprints.
The distinction of impure and ordinary earth, rock, and
    sand is a
Judgment of good or bad that does not exist in my mind.
Everything is a pure and pristine enlightened field.
Only a few fortunate ones are able to see this.
Long ago, the great Padmasambhava's aspiration and mission

Was hidden in the heart center of the fresh, inner
luminosity aspect of enlightenment.
It was opened with the key to realization of emptiness-
awareness of the ultimate aspect of enlightenment.
In that same moment, 84,000 Dharma teachings were
understood, like knots unraveling.
Today the very fortunate ones gather here.
In the near future, everyone will join together at the
Copper-Colored Palace.
Surrounded by clouds of awareness holders and dakinis,
I aspire to see the face of the great Padmasambhava![81]

THE TREASURE CHESTS AT
CHIMPUK HERMITAGE

Chimpuk Hermitage is a sacred place where Padmasambhava and many great practitioners of the past meditated and bestowed blessings. Jigme Phuntsok Rinpoche and his entourage were on their way there when a fierce demoness with disheveled face and exposed fangs suddenly appeared, trying to create trouble. Jigme Phuntsok Rinpoche manifested the look of wrathful Padmasambhava and harshly scolded the demoness, "You haven't received any teachings from Padmasambhava, nor have you ever seen him in person. You just roam about bringing harm to others and spend your days committing wrongdoings. Now you even want to bring me, a tantric yogi, obstacles. You will never succeed! Today I will feed you the food of bodhichitta and trap you under the ground for nine years." Jigme Phuntsok Rinpoche subdued the fierce demoness with wrathful methods and commanded her to take the vows of never again committing any wrongdoing and of protecting the Dharma. At the same time, he composed a demon-subduing sadhana.

After that, Jigme Phuntsok Rinpoche arrived at Chimpuk Hermitage. A dharmapala miraculously gave him a treasure chest that contained Padmasambhava's tantric work summarizing the pith instructions of the generation stage, the completion stage, and the Great Perfection. Padmasambhava composed the texts with the intention of dispelling calamities in the degenerate time and then concealed the terma in a chest shaped like an auspicious conch shell. He gave it to Yeshe Tsogyal and told her, "In the future, the incarnation of my heart-son Nanam Dorjé Dudjom will come to the sacred Chimpuk Hermitage with his entourage. At that time, the dharmapala will give him this treasure chest in person."

Several days later, Jigme Phuntsok Rinpoche called Khenpo Chöpa to his side and showed him the treasure chest, saying, "Today you must find a treasure chest similar to this one. Please do not return before you have found it." Khenpo Chöpa searched everywhere, eventually obtaining the chest from a female retreatant in Padmasambhava's meditation cave who was said to be an emanation of Yeshe Tsogyal. Jigme Phuntsok Rinpoche did not fully reveal the tantric texts sealed within the two treasure chests because the timing and conditions had not yet ripened; he disclosed and recorded only *The Sadhana of Kurukulla Practice* and *The Sadhana of the Wrathful Padmasambhava Practice*. Reciting the first sadhana can help practitioners uphold pure precepts. Reciting the second one can eliminate obstacles on the path.

Jigme Phuntsok Rinpoche's receiving of the two terma chests at Chimpuk Hermitage was long ago prophesied by Tertön Dribdral Rigpé Dorjé:

> At the sacred place of Padmasambhava, owing to the power of his aspiration in the previous life, albeit not requesting it, he will effortlessly receive terma objects and precious items. He will reveal the secret meaning of the termas truthfully. With his accumulated merit and aspirational power, he will be reborn in the Glorious Copper-Colored Mountain.

VISITS TO MONASTERIES IN U-TSANG

On his way home from Samye Monastery and Lhasa, Jigme Phuntsok Rinpoche visited several monasteries and sacred sites. First, he accepted an invitation to visit the renowned Drigung Monastery of the Kagyu lineage. As he slowly marched through the impressive welcoming crowd of the sangha, Jigme Phuntsok Rinpoche suddenly noticed the great Kagyu dharmapala Achi Chökyi Drolma, with her blue body and red hair, coming to greet him in the midst of a blazing fire and swift winds. Many others also witnessed miraculous signs on the spot at the same time. Instantly, Jigme Phuntsok Rinpoche composed *The Sadhana of Achi Chökyi Drolma* and said to the monastery's sangha, "If the Kagyu sangha can recite this sadhana regularly in the future, the Dharma teachings from your lineage will continuously flourish."

After that, Jigme Phuntsok Rinpoche went to the sacred mountains of the three principal dharmapalas of the Nyingma lineage. With the intention of spreading the Nyingma teachings widely across the world, he recited the prayers for dharmapalas and bestowed the empowerment of the dharmapalas on his disciples, telling them, "In today's time of five degenerations, it is hard to withstand the forceful adversities and demonic obstacles on your own. Thus, we must rely on the protection and blessing of dharmapalas who possess the power of wisdom. Likewise, to make the Dharma flourish, we especially need the full support of the dharmapalas. Therefore, I wish that, from now on, all of you will always pray to dharmapalas, so that you can dispel all obstacles and create favorable conditions in your practicing and propagating the Dharma."

Later, when Jigme Phuntsok Rinpoche passed Nyetang, a place where Atisha (982–1054) stayed after coming to Tibet, a large group of monks came forth to make an offering of food to him. During the meal, Jigme Phuntsok Rinpoche said to the monks, "Last night I dreamed that Lama Dromtönpa (1005–1064) offered me food, so I presume that the emanation of Dromtönpa must be among you. I should ask for blessings from him." After the meal, Jigme Phuntsok Rinpoche got up and asked the monks to touch the crown of his head to bestow him blessings. The monks were awestruck and immediately stepped back in embarrassment. Jigme Phuntsok Rinpoche went up to each of them and touched their hands with his head respectfully. They were flabbergasted and bent over as far as they could in return.

One day, Jigme Phuntsok Rinpoche and his entourage arrived at a Sakya monastery. When they entered the shrine hall, they saw a high throne. Jigme Phuntsok Rinpoche asked the monastery's incense master, "Do I need to sit on this throne?" The incense master looked a bit embarrassed and apologized, "When the Panchen Lama was here, he just bowed respectfully to the throne and didn't sit on it." Jigme Phuntsok Rinpoche said with a smile, "Very well then. Had I sat on the throne, I would have to reincarnate once in the Sakya lineage." After leaving, Jigme Phuntsok Rinpoche explained to his entourage, "At the age of eighteen or nineteen, when I was studying at Sershul, once when the Sakya lama Künga Sönam Rinpoche was bestowing me with the empowerment of *The Vajra Curtain Tantra*, he told me, 'You shall uphold the Sakya teachings, assume the role of a lineage holder, and widely propagate the Sakya teachings.' He thus entrusted me with this formidable responsibility at that time. I thought he was implying that I would have to reincarnate once in the Sakya lineage. But, given the omen that occurred today, it seems that this reincarnation is no longer necessary."

THE STORY OF A
BLACK GOAT

The great Jigme Phuntsok Rinpoche not only benefited innumerable human beings with the Dharma but also often transmitted oral teachings to the animals around him, giving them the chance to be liberated. One of these fortunate animals was a black mountain goat that had been following Jigme Phuntsok Rinpoche everywhere since its birth. The goat was very gentle and obedient to him. It always slept by the side of Jigme Phuntsok Rinpoche's pillow at night. Even when it had become a big adult goat, it was still very loyal to him. No matter where Jigme Phuntsok Rinpoche went, it was always willing to carry his load.

Jigme Phuntsok Rinpoche treated this goat with great lovingkindness and often offered it oral transmissions of Sutrayana and Vajrayana teachings, including the complete texts of the most profound *Four Parts of Heart Essence* and *The Seven Treasuries*. After being with Jigme Phuntsok Rinpoche for sixteen years, the goat passed away peacefully. After its death, Jigme Phuntsok Rinpoche often thought of the goat, wondering where it had been reborn.

On the twenty-fourth day of the first Tibetan month in the earth snake year of 1989, at about five o'clock in the morning, Jigme Phuntsok Rinpoche woke up and started to meditate. Suddenly he saw colorful lights, in the middle of which a cute child was walking toward him. The youngster, whose hair was knotted and who was dressed in white, respectfully bowed to Jigme Phuntsok Rinpoche and chanted the following stanza:

The treasure of powerful speech who fearlessly teaches,
    debates, and composes,
You have perfected the Threefold Training[82] and attained
    supreme wisdom,
You are the source of boundless benefit and happiness, like a
    wish-fulfilling jewel,
To you my supreme glorious master, I supplicate.

After chanting it three times, the youngster continued, "Do you recognize me? I am the black goat you used to have! In the past, you often transmitted the profound Sutrayana and Vajrayana teachings to my ears and granted me blessings with great kindness and compassion. Because of this, I was reborn into the Realm of Shambhala after my life as a goat and became an exceptionally smart bilingual parrot. I could fully understand the teachings given by Rigden Magagpa.[83] One month ago, I was reborn in the Eastern Land of Manifest Joy after my life as a parrot, and now dwell in the presence of Bodhisattva Jikpa Kunkyob,[84] who is in fact Mipham Rinpoche. I now come to pay my respects to you. May you live a long life! May your Dharma activities flourish in all ten directions!" Having said all this, he turned into a ball of light and disappeared.

Great faith and joy arose in Jigme Phuntsok Rinpoche's heart. In case he ever forgot the details of this encounter, he picked up his pen and wrote the following stanzas:

Today I heard that in the Eastern Land of Manifest Joy,
You, the incomparably kind master Mipham Rinpoche,
Have become the invincible protector named Protecting All
    from Fear,
And are now expounding the vast and profound teachings
To your pure assembly of countless bodhisattvas.

I am now immersed in samsara,
Amid the ordinary beings with inferior karma,

And constantly suffer sickness, demonic forces, and
    adversity.
When I am thinking of this,
A mix of sorrow and joy arises in me.
From the bottom of my heart, not merely from my lips,
The only thing I want to do is benefit beings and spread the
    Dharma.
I must accomplish the goal of benefiting beings
    wholeheartedly.

However, honorable master, don't you know that I am
    powerless?
Nowadays in the Land of Snows,
Although many people are teaching or practicing the
    Dharma,
They are actually engaging in the eight worldly concerns.
Those who practice the true Dharma are as rare as daytime
    stars.
When thinking of this, my heart aches.

All beings that live on the earth
Are burdened by unbearable suffering,
And continue to generate more causes of suffering.
How can you, the compassionate Protector, take this?
For all sentient beings that establish a connection with me,
Please guide them to the pure realm.
Please transform appearances of the prevalent five
    degenerations
In accordance with those of the Golden Age[85] of the past.

From now through all successive lives,
May you, the father, always accept us with joy,
Teach according to beings' wishes and interests,
And offer a happy banquet of the profound Dharma.

To instill strong interest and appreciation in his disciples toward listening to the Dharma teachings, Jigme Phuntsok Rinpoche publicly shared this story with the sangha.

CAVES IN NEPAL

Nepal is a sacred land of Buddhism where Padmasambhava and many other great vidyadharas have practiced and propagated Vajrayana teachings. Jigme Phuntsok Rinpoche chose to stop here with his entourage on their way to India in 1990 at the invitation of the great Penor Rinpoche[86] (1932–2009). During his stay in Nepal, Jigme Phuntsok Rinpoche accepted invitations from Urgyen Dongak Chöling, the monastery of the second Dudjom Rinpoche (1904–1987); Shechen Tennyi Dargyeling, the monastery of Dilgo Khyentse Rinpoche (1910–1991); and other monasteries. In these monasteries, Jigme Phuntsok Rinpoche gave teachings and bestowed empowerments. He also took a pilgrimage to the temple of Tham Bahi, which is said to have been constructed for Atisha by a Nepalese king. The temple houses the four volumes of the *Prajnaparamita Sutra* that Nagarjuna brought to the human realm from the palace of the Naga king.

One day, Jigme Phuntsok Rinpoche visited Yanglesho Cave with his seven companions. On seeing the enchanting scenery, Jigme Phuntsok Rinpoche felt very inspired and entered the nondual, luminous state of indivisible purity and equality. For the Nepalese and Tibetan Buddhists on the site, Jigme Phuntsok Rinpoche sang the following vajra song that spontaneously arose in his mind:

> The embodiment of all buddhas' missions, brave Manjushri,
> Please remain at my heart center in the fresh, inner
>   luminosity aspect of enlightenment.
> Accompanied by the blessing of wisdom luminosity,
> Please send forth great blessing and enlightened mind.
> When I arrive at the sacred place of Yanglesho, Nepal,

All experiences of impure distortion clear like a
   cloudless sky.
Not just temporarily seeing enlightened images through
   effort,
I directly see the face of ultimate enlightenment.
Here, at this very moment, everything is one taste of
   completely perfect emptiness-awareness.
Free from all hopes and fears of samsara and nirvana,
When the yogi free of delusions happily relaxes,
It simultaneously opens a hundred doors of perfect memory,
   wisdom, and courage.
Laypeople seek happiness in this life while
Monks seek happiness in the next life.
They are equally bound, but in iron or golden chains.
For both, it is hard to go beyond the narrow path of hope
   and fear.
Previously, the five poisons appeared like enemies.
Today, they are completely pure within
   emptiness-awareness.
By abandoning the meaningless and tiresome four sessions
   of meditation practice,
The yogi, who realizes all is illusion, happily sleeps in a
   comfortable bed.
Long ago, in this place, Manjushri-Padmasambhava
Reached great enlightenment directly.
Right now, his children and I follow his footsteps.
I release the knots of hope for other introductions or
   teachings.
The seven who accompany me to this place
Enjoy the legacy left by the founding fathers of the lineage.
Journey through the four stages of awareness holders like
   the flight of the garuda!
Become the captain helping all beings throughout the
   universe![87]

Then Jigme Phuntsok Rinpoche went to the nearby Asura Cave, where Padmasambhava had meditated and attained the level of *mahamudra vidyadhara*.[88] At this sacred site, Jigme Phuntsok Rinpoche directly perceived the purity of all appearances and fully realized the nature of great purity and equality in all phenomena. The scenes from his former life as Nepal's King Jinamitra appeared clearly in his mind, as well as the scenes when Padmasambhava transmitted the supreme teaching on the subjugation practice of Vajrakilaya at this very place. Immediately, from the ocean of his sublime wisdom, Jigme Phuntsok Rinpoche revealed the mind terma *The Neck-Pouch Vajrakilaya Practice*. The text of this Vajrakilaya practice was composed by Padmasambhava and is the most supreme practice to dispel obstacles. Padmasambhava had prophesied,

I, Padmasambhava, a self-manifested buddha, now entrust you, Jinamitra, with this quintessence of all the Vajrakilaya tantric practices. Please do not forget to practice it. In the degenerate age of the future, your honorable incarnation will reveal this practice and widely propagate it. Samaya!

Later in India, the honorable Gyalwa Rinpoche wrote a lineage prayer titled *The Swift Infusion of Blessings* for this Vajrakilaya practice.

Pilgrimage to the
Three Great Stupas

During Jigme Phuntsok Rinpoche's stay in Kathmandu, the capital city of Nepal, in addition to the sacred meditation sites, he also made pilgrimages to the three great stupas. Before circumambulating the stupas, Jigme Phuntsok Rinpoche said to his disciples, "The stupa is the embodiment of all the buddhas' wisdom. Buddha Shakyamuni once said, 'There is no difference between making an offering to me right now and making an offering to my stupa with a pure and devoted heart in the future.' Circumambulating a stupa can eradicate obscurations accumulated over many lifetimes through negative actions, as well as bring boundless merit. In Nepal, there are many sacred stupas full of blessing power, among which three are especially well-known. In the past, King Trisong Detsen visited Nepal especially for pilgrimages to these three stupas; therefore, we should appreciate this opportunity."

In late June of 1990, Jigme Phuntsok Rinpoche visited Swayambhunath Stupa, which is considered one of the world's most ancient stupas. It is said that, when the human lifespan was ten thousand years, from the sublime wisdom of all the buddhas a one-foot-high crystal stupa appeared spontaneously. It emerged in the middle of the ocean that covered that entirety of Nepal at the time of Buddha Krakucchanda.[89] Then, at the time of Buddha Kanakamuni,[90] this stupa was called the Stupa of Excellent Speech in Dharmadhatu. During the time of Buddha Kashyapa,[91] Master Shantashri built a larger stupa encasing the crystal one to better protect it; this stupa is today as majestic as ever.

The Vasubandhu Stupa is located near Swayambhunath Stupa. It enshrines the relics of Vasubandhu (fourth to fifth century), the influential Buddhist monk and philosopher. His connection to the stupa is described in this well-known story about his parinirvana:

> When Vasubandhu arrived at this very place, he happened to see a monk plowing land. The monk was dressed in layman's clothes and carrying a bottle of alcohol. Vasubandhu thought to himself, "Now it is indeed the degenerate time!" Struck by great sadness, he soon entered parinirvana. His stupa was later built at the very spot where he passed away.

In front of the Vasubandhu Stupa, Jigme Phuntsok Rinpoche lamented, "As monastics, we should focus on hearing, contemplating, and meditating on the Dharma. We should abstain from worldly preoccupations such as farming and trading. Didn't Vasubandhu, who was often regarded as the second Buddha, manifest his death out of aversion upon seeing a monk plowing land?"

Jigme Phuntsok Rinpoche resided at Dzimé Chölhé Zongnang Monastery near the Boudhanath Stupa during his stay in Kathmandu. Boudhanath Stupa is said to have been built by the previous incarnations of Padmasambhava, Shantarakshita, and King Trisong Detsen when they were born as the three sons of a poultry-farmer mother, Jadzimo. In that lifetime, they aspired to propagate the Dharma together in Tibet.

During his stay at Dzimé Chölhé Zongnang Monastery, Jigme Phuntsok Rinpoche ardently recited three hundred thousand times the following prayer in praise of Manjushri:

> Noble Vajra Manjushri,
> I earnestly pray to you:
> Please grant me the blessing
> That supreme wisdom permeates my mind.

On the day that he completed his recitations, people noticed a beam of white light from the top of Boudhanath Stupa shining directly into Jigme Phuntsok Rinpoche's room. All witnesses of this light beam developed great faith in him. Jigme Phuntsok Rinpoche said to his entourage, "Today I've just finished reciting three hundred thousand times the prayer in praise of Manjushri. Now let's circumambulate Boudhanath Stupa."

When circumambulating the stupa, Jigme Phuntsok Rinpoche told his entourage, "It is very important to make an aspiration. No matter what good deeds we undertake, we should always be motivated to do so with vast aspirations. While circumambulating this stupa, we should aspire to be reborn in the Blissful Pure Land of Amitabha. Do not make any unwholesome aspiration; otherwise, it will be just like the yak who made an evil aspiration when the previous incarnations of Padmasambhava and others were constructing this stupa, and later became the demonic king Langdarma!"[92]

After circumambulating Boudhanath Stupa, Jigme Phuntsok Rinpoche walked into a Buddhist statue store. He instantly noticed an extremely majestic statue of Manjushri on the counter. He gazed at the statue for a long time, then rubbed his eyes and continued staring at it. His attendants were puzzled and looked at him in confusion. Jigme Phuntsok Rinpoche joyfully explained, "When I first entered the store, I was immediately attracted by this Manjushri statue. Suddenly I found that the statue was smiling at me. I suspected it was a hallucination due to my defective eyesight. Thus, I rubbed my eyes and checked the statue again. Then I saw a ray of light emit from the heart of the statue and enter directly into my own heart. I would like to have this statue."

It turned out that the statue was not for sale. However, after much persuasion from Jigme Phuntsok Rinpoche's disciples, the shopkeeper finally agreed to sell it, which made Jigme Phuntsok Rinpoche very happy. He sang the following stanzas on the spot:

Forever residing in the sacred Mount Wutai,
Embodying the wisdom of tens of thousands of bodhisattvas,

Including the Eight Great Ones,[93]
Noble Vajra Manjushri, to you I prostrate!

I am a beginner tormented by obscurations,
But thankfully I have your skillful, compassionate
   protection.
This cast statue offers me great comfort.
No one can ever measure your great kindness and profound
   qualities.

In order to please you, the father,
I will undertake the bodhisattva's ocean-like deeds
Until the end of the boundless expanse of space,
To repay your limitless great kindness.

Since then, this Manjushri statue was referred to as the "speaking
Manjushri" or the "Dharma-wheel Manjushri," and was always at
the side of Jigme Phuntsok Rinpoche.

Later in Nepal, Jigme Phuntsok Rinpoche went to the sacred
pilgrimage site of Namo Buddha, where, according to the *Sutra
of the Wise and the Foolish*, one of Buddha Shakyamuni's former
incarnations offered his own body to a tiger. At that time, this
incarnation was born as a prince and offered his own body to a
starving tigress with five newborn cubs. His two elder brothers
were struck with grief after learning that their youngest brother
had fed himself to the tigress. They collected his remains of bones
and hair and built a stupa in remembrance of his selfless deed.

Recalling the enormously compassionate actions of the Buddha's previous incarnations when he was still on the bodhisattva's
path, Jigme Phuntsok Rinpoche started shedding tears and said,
"In his previous lives, our great teacher Buddha Shakyamuni gave
up his own body on countless occasions to benefit living beings of
the turbid time. We Mahayanists should follow his footsteps and
engage in the bodhisattva's deeds.[94] First of all, we should practice
generosity."

AUSPICIOUS KARMIC CONNECTIONS
WITH GYALWA RINPOCHE

The current Gyalwa Rinpoche, who is believed to be the emanation of Bodhisattva Avalokiteshvara, had an extraordinary karmic connection with the great Jigme Phuntsok Rinpoche in many past lifetimes. According to historical accounts, the Gyalwa Rinpoches throughout history had to rely on the tantric teachings of Padmasambhava and termas revealed by great tertöns in order to expand Dharma activities and dispel obstacles. The Fifth Gyalwa Rinpoche Ngawang Lobsang Gyatso (1617–1682) followed the great Tertön Minling Terchen Gyurme Dorjé (1646–1714) as his scripture teacher and transmitted and entrusted his revealed termas to Tertön Pema Trinlé—a former incarnation of Jigme Phuntsok Rinpoche. The Seventh Gyalwa Rinpoche Kalzang Gyatso (1708–1757) followed Tertön Dakpo Drodul. Due to these karmic connections, the past Gyalwa Rinpoches prolonged their lives and had successful Dharma activities.

Later, some rulers in the Tibetan empire exercised favoritism toward their own lineage and opposed the then Gyalwa Rinpoche's choice of following Nyingma teachers and studying the tantric teachings of the Nyingma lineage. As a result, several succeeding incarnations encountered great obstacles in their lifespan and Dharma activities.

Knowing these causes and conditions, the Thirteenth Gyalwa Rinpoche Thubten Gyatso followed the great Tertön Lerab Lingpa, the immediate preceding incarnation of the great Jigme Phuntsok Rinpoche, and respectfully received his Nyingma empowerments and tantric teachings. Thubten Gyatso especially focused on propagating *The Most Secret Sword of Vajrakilaya*, a terma revealed by Lerab Lingpa. In 1928, the year of the earth dragon of the sixteenth Rabjung cycle,[95] Tertön Lerab Lingpa revealed the wish-fulfilling life-force stone of Vajravarahi and Hayagriva[96] from a rock, which he offered to Thubten Gyatso. Because of this, Thubten Gyatso's lifespan was extended, his Dharma activities accelerated, and his religious and political reigns pervaded the Land of Snows like sunshine and moonlight.

Coincidentally, in 1988, the year of the earth dragon of the seventeenth Rabjung cycle, when the great Jigme Phuntsok Rinpoche was expounding tantric teachings to over one thousand monastics on the Tibetan Plateau, the following profound stanza spontaneously arose from his pristine awareness:

> When the thunder peals in the sky,
> And peacocks dance on the earth,
> May you bring the rain of auspicious messages,
> Which produces luxuriant leaves and abundant fruits.

Jigme Phuntsok Rinpoche then offered a white khata to Khenpo Namdrol, who was visiting the Land of Snows from India. When he returned to India, Khenpo Namdrol went to Drepung Monastery to offer one of Jigme Phuntsok Rinpoche's works to the honorable Gyalwa Rinpoche, who happily received it with both hands, touched it with the crown of his head, and prayed, "May I meet the great Jigme Phuntsok Rinpoche soon."

Soon after, Gyalwa Rinpoche said to Penor Rinpoche, the director of Namdroling Monastery in India, "The great Jigme Phuntsok Rinpoche, who is the incarnation of Tertön Lerab Lingpa—the scripture teacher of my immediate predecessor—is now propagating the Dharma in the Land of Snows. It will be of great benefit to the Dharma activities if you can invite him to India. I myself will also request his empowerment and teaching. You are a great master with faith, good character, and pure precepts, and also my close and loyal friend. Therefore, I entrust you with this mission." Penor

Rinpoche gladly agreed and sent a delegate to Sertar to officially invite Jigme Phuntsok Rinpoche to India. Due to his busy schedule and health problems, Jigme Phuntsok Rinpoche was unable to set out on the trip right away. But, in 1990, with the blessings of the Three Jewels, Jigme Phuntsok Rinpoche and his entourage successfully received travel permits and visas. Eventually, they arrived in New Delhi, the capital of India, as planned.

During his stay in India, Jigme Phuntsok Rinpoche received wholehearted welcomes from many monasteries and Buddhist communities. He also visited famous temples, the royal palace, and a few world-renowned tourist attractions. July is very hot and humid in India, and it was challenging for Jigme Phuntsok Rinpoche and his entourage to adapt to the tropical climate. One day, in the hotel room where Jigme Phuntsok Rinpoche was staying, to his ears the noise of the hotel air conditioner became the enchanting sound of the recitation of *In Praise of Manjushri* for over an hour.

A few days later, Gyalwa Rinpoche sent a car to New Delhi to pick up Jigme Phuntsok Rinpoche and his entourage. Having received the legal documents and full permission from the Chinese Embassy in India, Jigme Phuntsok Rinpoche left for northern India, where the honorable Gyalwa Rinpoche resides.

Meeting the Honorable Gyalwa Rinpoche

The honorable Gyalwa Rinpoche's place is located about 480 kilometers from New Delhi. It is surrounded by cedar forests in the foothills of the Himalayas, with distant views of the snowy mountains. Visitors are often impressed by its pleasant climate; it remains cool and refreshing in summer, bringing comfort to those—like Jigme Phuntsok Rinpoche—who have had enough of India's tropical heat.

On July 16, 1990, Jigme Phuntsok Rinpoche arrived at Namgyal Monastery to a grand welcoming ceremony with the honorable Gyalwa Rinpoche offering a khata and a golden statue of Buddha Shakyamuni. Although it was their first encounter, it was as if they were two brothers finally reuniting after a long separation. How joyful they were! That afternoon, Jigme Phuntsok Rinpoche gave Gyalwa Rinpoche the empowerment of his recently revealed terma *The Neck-Pouch Vajrakilaya Practice*. Afterward, the two masters held hands and walked to Gyalwa Rinpoche's living room, where they eagerly recounted the karmic connection they shared in propagating the Dharma and benefiting sentient beings together in past lifetimes.

The following day, owing to a special cause, a long-life prayer for the honorable Gyalwa Rinpoche arose from Jigme Phuntsok Rinpoche's wisdom mind. That afternoon, to promote world peace and the propagation of the Dharma, the two masters held a grand tsok offering ceremony in the main hall of Namgyal Monastery. The tsok offering was based on Tertön Lerab Lingpa's terma *The Most Secret Sword of Vajrakilaya*. Among the attendees were the sangha members of Namgyal Monastery and Nechung Monastery, as well as many local and international Buddhist devotees. It was quite a spectacular event. The two great masters sat majestically on their respective thrones, each holding a phurba, which aroused reverence in the hearts of the attendees. At times, they appeared wrathfully with fierce expressions and gestures to subdue evil demons and tirthikas. At other times, they resumed their compassionate appearances and gave teachings. Accordingly, the attendees felt awestruck one moment and blissful the next. They prayed for the blessings of the buddhas of the ten directions, so that all beings would be able to bathe in the sunshine of the Dharma, drink the nectar of the wondrous teachings, be freed from suffering and enjoy happiness, and eventually attain the ultimate enlightenment.

On July 18, a sadhana of the Vajrakilaya fire offering[97] appeared in Jigme Phuntsok Rinpoche's pristine awareness. He immediately shared the terma aloud, and Gyalwa Rinpoche wrote it down accordingly. It is truly remarkable that Gyalwa Rinpoche could already fluently recite the section of the auspicious verse in this newly revealed terma more than a decade ago.

On July 19, Jigme Phuntsok Rinpoche offered the honorable Gyalwa Rinpoche a Manjushri statue—the terma object he specifically revealed for Gyalwa Rinpoche at the Narayana Cave of Mount Wutai. Gyalwa Rinpoche was delighted and offered Jigme Phuntsok Rinpoche a golden mandala set and silver coins[98] in return. Jigme Phuntsok Rinpoche then gave Gyalwa Rinpoche the empowerment of *The Great Perfection of the Peaceful Manjushri*. Around noon, the two great masters enjoyed lunch at Gyalwa Rinpoche's new living quarters, during which they talked about their supreme affinity with each other in past lives as teacher and disciple and as sovereign and minister. Gyalwa Rinpoche sincerely said, "You are the protector of the Dharma in the Land of Snows! If you encounter obstacles in the future, please do not be deterred by them. You must remain steadfast like a towering pine tree in a blizzard. I sincerely wish you live long and widely benefit beings."

Then he offered Jigme Phuntsok Rinpoche a precious statue of Amitayus, the Buddha of Eternal Life.

On July 20, at the invitation of Nechung Monastery, Jigme Phuntsok Rinpoche went to bestow the Vajrakilaya empowerment. When he was reciting the prayer to invoke the deity, Dharmapala Dorjé Drakden suddenly appeared.[99] Dorjé Drakden disclosed his karmic connections with Lerab Lingpa, prophesied Jigme Phuntsok Rinpoche's future Dharma activities, and suggested, "Padmasambhava has always been caring for and blessing you in the Dharmadhatu. You should subdue all evil beings and demons with the wrathful practice of Vajrakilaya." The Auspicious Goddess and other dharmapalas also appeared. They validated Jigme Phuntsok Rinpoche as the true manifestation of Padmasambhava and a compassionate protector for beings in this degenerate age.

On July 21, for the whole day, Jigme Phuntsok Rinpoche and the honorable Gyalwa Rinpoche discussed several difficult issues in the Sutrayana and Vajrayana teachings.

On July 22, upon the sincere supplication of Jigme Phuntsok Rinpoche and his entourage, Gyalwa Rinpoche bestowed on them the empowerment of his predecessor Ngawang Lobsang Gyatso's terma *The Complete Collection of the Innermost Essence of Mind Practices*. Afterward, Jigme Phuntsok Rinpoche bestowed the Vajrakilaya empowerment on the Namgyal Monastery sangha. In return, the sangha made a special Dharma offering with their remarkable debate. Jigme Phuntsok Rinpoche was very pleased and praised the sangha's exceptional eloquence.

On July 24, Jigme Phuntsok Rinpoche taught Patrul Rinpoche's *The Three Words That Strike the Vital Point* to Gyalwa Rinpoche. Then the two great masters engaged in a discussion about the similarities and differences between the *Guhyasamaja Tantra* and the *Kalachakra Tantra*, as well as between the two subschools— Svatantrika (Autonomy) and Prasangika (Consequence)—of the Madhyamika school (the Middle Way). Both masters offered a detailed analysis on the topics based on various Buddhist scriptures.

July 25 is the fourth day of the sixth Tibetan month, the day that Buddha Shakyamuni first turned the Wheel of Dharma. The two great masters generated the supreme bodhichitta together and recited *The King of Aspiration Prayers of Samantabhadra* in front of an ancient statue of Bodhisattva Avalokiteshvara, aspiring to benefit innumerable living beings. The honorable Gyalwa Rinpoche brought this Avalokiteshvara statue from the Tibetan Plateau to India. It is one of the five sacred statues from the Tibetan king Songtsen Gampo. Gyalwa Rinpoche treasures the statue dearly and considers it his only true companion. After making the aspiration, owing to the dependent arising, the honorable Gyalwa Rinpoche offered Jigme Phuntsok Rinpoche a pure-gold Dharma Wheel decorated with many precious gemstones, wishing Jigme Phuntsok Rinpoche a long life and that he always turn the Wheel of Dharma for the benefit of sentient beings.

Later, when Jigme Phuntsok Rinpoche traveled to southern India to bestow empowerments at several monasteries, including Gyudmed Monastery where Gyalwa Rinpoche joined him from northern India. During a Dharma assembly at Gyudmed Monastery, Gyalwa Rinpoche introduced Jigme Phuntsok Rinpoche to the crowd in a tone of appreciation, "Jigme Phuntsok Rinpoche is the incarnation of Tertön Lerab Lingpa, who was the scripture teacher of my immediate predecessor Ngawang Lobsang Gyatso; he is the present-day throne holder of the Nyingma lineage. Therefore, I specifically invited him here. It is truly auspicious for all of you present here today to have the opportunity to see him in person." Afterward, Gyalwa Rinpoche bestowed the empowerments of Avalokiteshvara and Guhyasamaja upon the crowd. During their stay in the monastery, Jigme Phuntsok Rinpoche offered Gyalwa Rinpoche the empowerment of Buddha Amitayus using a sadhana titled *The Miraculous Vase of Nectar*.

In the following days, renowned masters and abbots from the Geluk, Kagyu, Sakya, and other Tibetan Buddhist lineages in India invited Jigme Phuntsok Rinpoche to give teachings. At the time, there were slight disagreements among these traditions.

Jigme Phuntsok Rinpoche's visit helped establish a bridge of communication for different lineages and fostered harmonious relationships among them.

Buddhists across India praised Jigme Phuntsok Rinpoche as the pivotal pillar of Dharma in the Tibetan region. When local Tibetans heard that Jigme Phuntsok Rinpoche came to India from their homeland, they were overwhelmed with emotion and could not wait to pay their respects. Seeing Jigme Phuntsok Rinpoche in person was like lost children being reunited with their loving mother. The mixture of nostalgia and joy they experienced is difficult to put into words.

Later, Jigme Phuntsok Rinpoche took a pilgrimage to Tso Pema, the sacred "Lotus Lake" in North India. According to the *Biography of Padmasambhava*, when Padmasambhava was in the land of Zahor, the king attempted to burn him alive. Padmasambhava performed a miracle, transforming the funeral pyre into a lake, and was found sitting, cool and relaxed, on a lotus blossom in its center. This lake was thus named the Lotus Lake and today attracts many pilgrims. Normally, the lotus roots are embedded in the mud at the bottom of the lake, but when Jigme Phuntsok Rinpoche approached the lakeshore, several lotus roots miraculously floated up to the surface and gradually drifted toward him. Seeing this, the surrounding tourists were in awe. Jigme Phuntsok Rinpoche composed a prayer to Padmasambhava in the form of a vajra song. Afterward, he visited several nearby caves known for their blessing power.

PILGRIMAGES TO BUDDHIST
SACRED SITES IN INDIA

India holds profound significance in the hearts of Buddhists as the birthplace of Buddhism and the sacred land where Buddha Shakyamuni manifested the twelve deeds of enlightenment[100] in the human realm. Every faithful Buddhist aspires to make a pilgrimage to this sacred land, seeking to connect with the Buddha, whose presence is still felt at stupas, monasteries, and other sacred sites.

Following his trip to North India, Jigme Phuntsok Rinpoche proceeded to South India and primarily resided at Namdroling Monastery, where he spent nearly one month. He gave empowerments, such as *The Innermost Heart Drop of the Guru*, to Penor Rinpoche and a few thousand of his sangha members and taught *Beacon of Certainty* and other texts. His incisive teachings integrated many pith instructions, which received wholehearted appreciation and admiration from the audience, ranging from great masters, high tulkus, and eminent khenpos to ordinary monastics, who were all genuinely impressed by his profound wisdom and unparalleled eloquence. Here, Jigme Phuntsok Rinpoche was awarded the highest honorary degree recognized in the Tibetan Buddhist community—an honorary doctorate degree in Buddhism—in recognition of his proficiency in both Sutrayana and Vajrayana teachings. Jigme Phuntsok Rinpoche also went to Sera Jey Monastery of the Geluk lineage to give the Nyingma teachings to over a thousand sangha members in the grand Dharma hall.

Jigme Phuntsok Rinpoche also visited museums, ancient temples, and other famous tourist attractions and made pilgrimages to each of the renowned Buddhist sacred sites in South India. He first visited the Nagarjuna Hill, where Nagarjuna, the founder of the Middle Way school, expounded teachings. Then he made a pilgrimage to Amaravati Stupa, where Buddha Shakyamuni taught the *Kalachakra Tantra*. At this site, Jigme Phuntsok Rinpoche spontaneously revealed *The Brief Practice of Kalachakra* out of his pristine awareness and gave the Kalachakra empowerment to his disciples and Buddhist devotees. He made an aspiration that all beings who established a connection with him at this site would be reborn into the Realm of Shambhala.

A few days later, Jigme Phuntsok Rinpoche started to make pilgrimages more widely across India. Specifically, in order, he visited the four famous Buddhist sites where Buddha Shakyamuni attained enlightenment, turned the Wheel of Dharma, passed into *mahaparinirvana*,[101] and was born. As said in the *Debate Sutra*:

> If one makes pilgrimages to these four sacred sites,
> Even one's five crimes with immediate retribution will be
> purified.

The first pilgrimage stop was Bodh Gaya, the site where Buddha Shakyamuni attained enlightenment, commemorated by the Mahabodhi Temple. There, Jigme Phuntsok Rinpoche led his disciples in reciting *The King of Aspiration Prayers of Samantabhadra* to make aspirations together. He also composed *The Sun of Samantabhadra's Realm: The Quintessence of Oceanic Prayers of Aspiration*.[102]

There is a statue known as the "Talking Tara" near the Mahabodhi Temple. It is said that when Atisha visited the Vajra Seat where Buddha Shakyamuni reached enlightenment, this statue tilted its head and spoke to him with a smile: "If you wish to quickly attain the perfect enlightenment, cultivating bodhichitta is the fastest path." That is how the statue got its name. When Jigme Phuntsok Rinpoche saw the Talking Tara statue, he immediately placed his ruby mala beads around her neck as an offering.

Miraculously, three years later, the same mala beads returned to his room at Larung Gar.

Jigme Phuntsok Rinpoche also visited the Nairanjana River,[103] where Buddha Shakyamuni spent six years doing ascetic practice. Jigme Phuntsok Rinpoche taught the merits of asceticism to the many Buddhists there. At the very place where Buddha Shakyamuni accepted a meal of milk-rice porridge from a milkmaid, thus ending his asceticism and enabling him to attain enlightenment, Jigme Phuntsok Rinpoche was expounding on the merits of offering, when a cute little monkey hopped over with a flower in its hands and offered it to him. Jigme Phuntsok Rinpoche gladly accepted the flower offering and recited prayers to dedicate the merit to the monkey.

Two days later, Jigme Phuntsok Rinpoche arrived at the sacred site of the Vulture Peak, where Buddha Shakyamuni turned the second Wheel of Dharma. At the foot of the mountain, Jigme Phuntsok Rinpoche said with a humorous expression, "When the Sixth Gyalwa Rinpoche came here, he saw the mountain covered with Buddhist scriptures. As for me, everything I am perceiving is luminosity, and I've truly experienced the state mentioned in the sutra—'The Buddha has no *parinirvana*; the Dharma never gets concealed.' You all can go to the mountain top. I'm staying here."

At Sarnath, or the Deer Park, where Buddha Shakyamuni turned the first Wheel of Dharma to the five disciples,[104] Jigme Phuntsok Rinpoche visited the Sarnath Museum and the Ashoka Pillar. Then he bestowed the empowerment of *The Wisdom Warrior Manjushri* on a Buddhist group mainly consisting of teachers and students from the Central Institute of Higher Tibetan Studies in Varanasi. Jigme Phuntsok Rinpoche delivered a talk that integrated Buddhism with science, catered to non-Buddhists and scholars in the audience.

At Kushinagar, where the Buddha passed into mahaparinirvana, Jigme Phuntsok Rinpoche, with tears in his eyes, said emotionally, "In order to help living beings generate aversion toward samsara and fully understand impermanence, the Buddha passed into parinirvana and his physical body entered the Dharmadhatu here, after the Buddha resided in this world for eighty-one years and spent forty-nine years teaching the Dharma. Therefore, we should not grasp onto anything as permanent."

The last sacred site that Jigme Phuntsok Rinpoche visited was Lumbini, the Buddha's birthplace. Today it is located in the Terai plains of southern Nepal. To lead erring beings onto the path of liberation, the great compassionate Buddha Shakyamuni descended into this world at this very spot. The moment he was born, he proclaimed, "In heaven and on earth, I alone am the World-Honored One." Recalling this, Jigme Phuntsok Rinpoche couldn't help but shed tears of reverence. With strong devotion in his heart, he placed his palms together and started to pray by chanting the name of Buddha Shakyamuni.

Many people visit these sacred sites with the lens of a tourist: they sightsee and take photos. Jigme Phuntsok Rinpoche and his entourage visited as Buddhist pilgrims: they focused on praying, prostration, circumambulation, making aspirations, and other devotional acts, which we Buddhists can emulate.

THE TRIP TO BHUTAN

As Bhutan used to be part of the Tubo Kingdom in Tibetan history, it still keeps many fine Tibetan traditions and remains a country where Buddhism flourishes to this day. In 1990, the year of the iron horse, Bhutan faced serious threat of foreign invasion. A small country like Bhutan could easily be annexed by a more powerful nation, but the blessings of the buddhas and bodhisattvas in this country are immeasurable and inconceivable. The terma revealed by Tertön Drukdra Dorjé states, "In the future, at the junction of a year of the sheep and a year of the horse, this country will face danger. If a noble emanation of Manjushri from the Tibetan region can be invited to come here, all calamities can be eliminated by his power."

When King Jigme Singye Wangchuck (b. 1955) learned that Jigme Phuntsok Rinpoche was a true emanation of Manjushri, he thought, "If we invite this eminent master to our country, he will surely dispel the present calamity and greatly contribute to the flourishing of Buddhism, the prosperity of the nation, and the well-being of the people." After consulting with the government officials, the king sent an official invitation letter to Jigme Phuntsok Rinpoche.

Jigme Phuntsok Rinpoche accepted the invitation and came to Thimphu, the capital city of Bhutan, and received a wholehearted welcome from the king; the lama of the royal family, Dilgo Khyentse Rinpoche; government officials; and many others. In Kyichu Lhakhang, a temple built by the Tibetan king Songtsen Gampo, Jigme Phuntsok Rinpoche gave the empowerments of *The Wrathful Padmasambhava*, *The Neck-Pouch Vajrakilaya*, and others to Dilgo Khyentse Rinpoche.

In Kyichu Lhakhang, King Jigme Singye Wangchuck, the king's

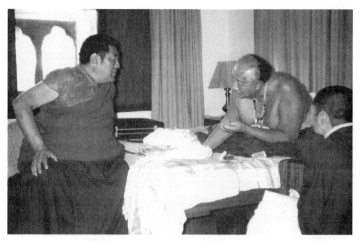

The great Jigme Phuntsok Rinpoche with
Dilgo Khyentse Rinpoche, 1990.

mother, and the queen met with Jigme Phuntsok Rinpoche. Here
is the paraphrase of Jigme Phuntsok Rinpoche's suggestion to the
king:

> Noble King, your status is as high as the sky; your sub-
> jects live a carefree, happy life and perform good deeds.
> The entire nation follows the profound teachings of
> Mahayana Buddhism, and your country's devotion to
> Buddhism is truly admirable. Your honorable country
> stands out strong like a majestic snow mountain.
>
> However, the outer circumstances of pleasure and
> pain are unpredictable, and threats from the scorching
> sun from the west[105] are imminent. There is a danger that
> the snow melts and becomes water. If you engage in the
> Padmasambhava and Vajrakilaya practices wholeheart-
> edly and gather vast accomplishments as your support,
> the majestic snow mountain will remain ever solid and
> stable. Due to his past malicious aspiration, someone
> intends to murder you when circumstances allow. Only

the mind emanation of Manjushri, the Wish-Fulfilling Jewel on the earth, can protect you.

From now on, you should uphold the golden victory banner of the Kagyu tradition and adorn it with the precious crown of the Nyingma tradition. By doing so, the state affairs and the Dharma in Bhutan will prosper like the waxing moon.

Later the calamity in Bhutan was eventually dispelled, quite possibly due to the blessing power of Jigme Phuntsok Rinpoche.

Afterward, Jigme Phuntsok Rinpoche went on pilgrimage to several Bhutanese sacred places. He first visited Paro Taktsang, also known as the Tiger's Nest, where Padmasambhava appeared as Dorjé Drolö[106] to subdue demons. Entering the meditation cave, Jigme Phuntsok Rinpoche revealed the mind terma *The Dorjé Drolö Practice* from his pristine awareness. He said, "Actually, during my vision, the dharmapala handed me nine volumes of *The Elaborated Sadhanas on the Wrathful Padmasambhava's Practices.* However, because the holder of this terma series is not present, plus some causes and conditions are missing, I only revealed the profound mind terma[107] and left the voluminous earth terma[108] unrevealed. This is also a good thing because by keeping the earth terma unrevealed for now, it can bring benefit to future beings in Bhutan. Therefore, I won't reveal the terma in this life. I will only do so in my next life." This story shows that Padmasambhava had personally instructed that many of his termas would be revealed by Jigme Phuntsok Rinpoche.

A few days later, on his way to Bumthang in central Bhutan, Jigme Phuntsok Rinpoche passed through Wangdue Phodrang, the place where King Gesar once defeated King Langshok. Scenes from his past life naturally surfaced in his mind. He told his entourage, "In those days when King Gesar and his troops went to Wangdue to subdue King Langshok, many nonhuman beings obstructed us and created many obstacles on our way. Now that I am setting foot on the land of Wangdue again, these nonhuman beings, out of their vengeance, will surely try to hinder me. Thus, we'd better be extra cautious."

As expected, not long after Jigme Phuntsok Rinpoche said so, dark clouds covered the sky, a heavy hailstorm suddenly hit the area, and mudslides occurred. Jigme Phuntsok Rinpoche manifested a wrathful appearance, sang a vajra song loudly, and chanted the subjugation mantra. Soon, the hail and floods stopped, and everything was back to normal.

In Bumthang near the Chumey Valley, Jigme Phuntsok Rinpoche visited a shrine hall owned by a local Buddhist devotee. The shrine hall housed the wooden phurba personally crafted by Tertön Nyangrel Nyima Özer (1124–1192). While Jigme Phuntsok Rinpoche was holding the phurba in his hand, the mind terma *The Brief Sadhana of the Eight Great Sadhana Teachings* spontaneously arose in his mind. The text was transcribed by his disciple right away and then preserved in an amulet box, with the instruction not to make it public for the next three years. Due to the absence of the right causes and conditions, this sadhana hasn't been made widely available.

Afterward, Jigme Phuntsok Rinpoche visited Kurjey Lhakhang, where Padmasambhava did a cave retreat. Jigme Phuntsok Rinpoche first paid homage to the rock where Padmasambhava left the imprint of his body. In the ancient hall of Dharmapala Tsiu Marpo, he recited the sadhana for the dharmapala and offered a khata to the dharmapala's statue.

On the way to Gangtey Monastery, Tsiu Marpo appeared by taking possession of a monk and requested an empowerment from Jigme Phuntsok Rinpoche. Hence, Jigme Phuntsok Rinpoche bestowed the Vajrakilaya empowerment on the dharmapala and a few disciples. Overjoyed, the dharmapala made future prophecies to Jigme Phuntsok Rinpoche and told him, "At any critical moment, if you call upon me, I will definitely come and assist you." As a result of this connection, Jigme Phuntsok Rinpoche composed a sadhana for the Dharmapala Tsiu Marpo out of his pristine awareness.

A Spiritual Journey to Small Tushita

Everyone experiences dreams. Yet ordinary people cannot roam freely in a buddha realm and converse with buddhas and bodhisattvas in a dream. The following account of one of Jigme Phuntsok Rinpoche's dreams is from his collective works.

At midnight on the first day of the tenth Tibetan month of the water monkey year of 1992, when I was half asleep in my bedroom, a lovely young man appeared before me. He seemed to be around sixteen years old, and his hair was tied into several knots like what some youngsters do nowadays. He was dressed in silk garments and adorned with precious jewelry. His exquisite and translucent appearance was captivating.

He said to me in a crisp voice, "Let's go outside and walk around together."

I replied, "I am seriously ill right now. My body feels very heavy, and I have great difficulty walking around. Who are you, anyway?"

"I am a longtime friend of yours. My name is Shyonu Khyenpa Dame.[109] You don't need to worry about a thing. If you cannot walk by yourself, I can carry you." Then he took my hand. Without thinking too much, I started to follow him.

We crossed many mountains that I had never seen before and arrived at a scenic mountain cave. I immediately noticed my root lama Thubga Rinpoche was sitting there. He appeared just as majestic as he did when he was approaching parinirvana. I was overwhelmed with excitement and devotion, and all my discursive thoughts halted instantly, leaving me stunned.

After I came back to my senses, I asked, "Dear Lama, didn't you pass into parinirvana a long time ago? Back then, when you parted from me, I was only twenty-four years old. Now I have already reached old age, and this illusory body of mine has become very ugly and feeble. Yet, you remain exactly the same as before, neither older nor younger. How is this possible?"

Thubga Rinpoche humorously replied, "This is 'All phenomena are devoid of inherent existence as they appear.' Don't tell me you don't understand this? Ha ha!"

I said in sadness, "My lama of great kindness, my mind is somewhat unsettled as I am tormented by heart disease. Especially now, I have contracted a severe and undiagnosed illness. May you please bless me by blowing air on me?"

With a tone of surprise, Thubga Rinpoche replied, "Oh! So, of all things, what concerns you most is your own illness, huh?" On hearing these words, I felt very embarrassed and said regretfully,

> Alas! I beseech my honorable protector of great
> compassion:
> Please look kindly upon me, a being with bad
> karma and inferior conditions.
> Even though I have long cultivated bodhichitta,
> I still focus on my own benefit. How
> embarrassing!

Saying this, I couldn't help but shed tears. Thubga Rinpoche lovingly comforted me, saying, "It is alright. On the path of cultivating bodhichitta, one must put on the armor of diligence and courage. Let us, as father and son, put our foreheads together, and I will recite an aspiration prayer for you":

> The only cause of all the virtues in samsara and
> nirvana
> Is the supreme jewel-like bodhichitta.
> May you, after generating bodhichitta
> effortlessly,
> Accomplish the activities of propagating the
> Dharma and benefiting beings.

While reciting the prayer, Thubga Rinpoche touched his head with mine with loving-kindness. I was quite moved, thinking, "I want to forever stay by my lama's side."

Just at this moment, the young boy was discontented and said to me, "Do not take what appears as what it is. Let's go! Let's go!" He then brought me to a dense forest where a delightful young crown prince was sitting in the center, surrounded by numerous *shravakas*,[110] *pratyeka-buddhas*,[111] and bodhisattvas.

I whispered to the young boy, asking, "What place is this? Who is the teacher? And where are his entourage members from?"

He answered, "This place is called the Small Tushita, and the teacher is the crown prince—the son of Bodhisattva Maitreya. All the entourage members are bodhisattvas who have only one more lifetime left before reaching Buddhahood. Although in the past they have made numerous vows before you and others to be reborn in the Pure Land of Amitabha, due to their karmic obscurations resulted from abandoning the Dharma and committing the crimes with immediate retribution, they were temporarily reborn here. Later, they will definitely be reborn in the Pure Land."

THE GOLDEN GARUDA — 151

I was quite puzzled, so I asked, "It is said that the celestial beings in the Realm of Desire have neither semen nor blood, so they can enjoy intersexual pleasure only through dispersing vital energy. If so, how is it possible that Maitreya has a son?"

The young boy reminded me, "Without causes and conditions, nothing arises, whereas with causes and conditions, things come into being. This is the reason, isn't it?"

Upon hearing this, I immediately realized that the young crown prince was the true Bodhisattva Maitreya, so I prostrated myself before him and prayed respectfully:

> Regent of the Buddha, protector of all sentient
> . beings,
> Who spontaneously manifests compassion at all
> times,
> The proponent of Dharma at this degenerate era
> and my only refuge,
> The youthful sublime one, I pay homage to you!

Then I asked, "Are the statements on generating bodhichitta that I proposed yesterday correct or not?"

Maitreya answered, "Regardless of a few minor flaws in the wording, the intended meaning you expressed is completely consistent with mine."

I asked again, "Tomorrow the learned sangha members will debate and discuss on the topic of 'Whether those on the path of joining generate conceptual constructions.' There are diverging opinions on this. What is the ultimate, definite answer to this?"

Maitreya laughed and said, "What is the use of studying and discussing the topic related to the conceptual thoughts on the path of joining? Even if one doesn't know this, it will not impede one's attainment of realization. Wouldn't it be better if one concentrates on the practice of Dzogchen? Ha ha, I'm just joking! As I've mentioned in my work,[112] 'The distinction of actor, action, and the object of action leads to cognitive obscurations.' If you can fully comprehend and integrate the teachings of this shastra, there is no longer anything difficult to understand. Regarding this, Haribhadra[113] has also provided detailed explanations, which you can always consult."

I continued to ask, "Regarding the hidden meaning of your *Ornament of Realizations*, Tibetans, the wise and the fool included, have their own opinions, and no consensus has been reached. May I please know the definite hidden meaning that you presented in this work?"

Maitreya kindly said, "It has been a long time since I wanted to proclaim it, but the opportune moment has not yet arrived, so I have been postponing it." After saying that, he touched my crown with his right hand to grant me blessing, and chanted the following stanza:

> May you, the man with the virtuous affinity,
> Come to Tushita not long from now,
> For when we gather with countless bodhisattvas,
> I shall impart to you this vast and profound
>   teaching.

After uttering these words, he disappeared.

The young boy, Shyonu Khyenpa Dame, escorted me back to my bed and said, "Now you sleep well, and do not forget the profound meaning of this journey. Please remember it!"

I woke up the next morning and still vividly remembered this spiritual journey I took in my dream.

FAILED TO OPEN THE TERMA GATEWAY

The extraordinary terma tradition is a particularly significant and integral part of the Nyingma lineage. Although the great Jigme Phuntsok Rinpoche revealed many termas throughout his life, his most important terma activity was to open the terma gateway located in the sacred Mountain Drongri. This was also his most important Dharma activity in this lifetime. If the terma gateway is opened successfully, tens of thousands of people will be able to directly go to the pure realm. Furthermore, it would also enable non-Buddhists, such as scientific researchers, to witness this substantial Buddhist mystery with their own eyes.

Padmasambhava made the following prophecy, as recorded in *The Clear Mirror of Illusions*:

> You, Nanam Dorjé Dudjom of today,
> In the future dragon year in Nyarong,
> Will reveal termas that can eliminate the calamities of the world.
> Your emanation, who will be born in a bird year in the east,
> Will reveal the termas if causes and conditions mature,
> Which can allow living beings of the turbid age
> To enter the pure realm without leaving their physical bodies behind.

Tertön Dribdral Rigpé Dorjé also prophesied:

> When a retreat center is built in Sertar near Mountain
> Drongri,
> And the red and white flowers blossom on the five snow
> mountains,
> You will open the thirteen terma gateways.

To open the thirteen gateways one by one, it is imperative to start with the terma gateway at the sacred Mountain Drongri. In other words, if the Drongri gateway fails to be opened, the rest of the terma gateways cannot be opened.

In 1992, the news that Jigme Phuntsok Rinpoche was to open the Drongri gateway on the tenth day of the tenth Tibetan month spread rapidly in all directions. It had become a major focus of attention in the Tibetan region, and people were really looking forward to this event. Jigme Phuntsok Rinpoche, with a resolute tone, said to a large crowd, "The opening of the Drongri terma gateway is of great importance, and its benefits are immeasurable. If successful, it will enable countless living beings to attain supreme achievement. If all the necessary causes and conditions are present but I fail to open the terma gateway, I am willing to crawl like a dog in front of the crowd. The prerequisite is that you need to gather all the favorable causes and conditions before the monkey month of the monkey year; otherwise, there is nothing I can do."

Just as a locked door requires a key to be opened, to unlock this terma gateway, Jigme Phuntsok Rinpoche had to first reveal the "key" that was concealed as a terma object. This terma key was hidden in a white lion-shaped rock at Mountain Drongri. Padmasambhava had already mentioned in his prophecy, "In order to get this key, it is crucial that all the favorable causes and conditions, such as the primary condition of opening up the road, are present."

Tertön Kunzang Nyima prophesied:

> The crown prince of Dharma from the Dakini realm,
> The Wish-Fulfilling Jewel[114] atop the heads of noble beings,

Now his aspirations from past lives have ripened.
In his hand he holds the thirteen terma gateways,
And he needs the auspicious key to open them.

During the degenerate time, demonic forces are too rampant, and they commit wrongdoings and create chaos everywhere. They set up obstacles by all means to impede activities that can benefit sentient beings. Padmasambhava prophesied, "During the process of accumulating favorable causes and conditions for opening this auspicious terma gateway, individuals possessed by demonic forces will create unfavorable conditions."

That was exactly what happened. A group of people possessed by demonic forces strongly opposed and sabotaged the necessary conditions needed to open the road to Mountain Drongri. As a result, the favorable causes and conditions to open the terma gateway were ruined. Despite the dedicated efforts of many great masters, government officials, and Buddhist devotees, it was impossible to get the terma key due to the collective karmic influence of sentient beings. The terma gateway couldn't be opened, which left people in great sorrow.

Jigme Phuntsok Rinpoche recalled his past lives and said to the crowd in tears,

> My original plan was to hear, contemplate, and meditate on the Dharma during my youth, to propagate the Dharma and reveal termas in my middle age, and to open the terma gateways in my old age. Opening the gateways would allow beings who don't trust the Dharma and who are hard to convince, especially scientific researchers, to witness the pure realm with their own eyes and to dispel their doubts and suspicion. It would also enable innumerable beings to go to the pure realm without leaving their physical bodies behind. In my past life, I made the vow in front of Padmasambhava to reveal termas. However, living beings in this turbid

time are too deficient in merit, so that such an auspicious terma gateway failed to be opened. This is truly heart-wrenching! I can hardly sleep and eat when thinking about it. At the present time, it is impossible to open the gateway. If all the favorable causes and conditions are present thirteen years from now, perhaps there will be another chance."

Regrettably, the favorable causes and conditions were not present thirteen years later, and therefore the terma gateway still has not been opened.

A few years after his attempt to open the gateway, Jigme Phuntsok Rinpoche said with deep sorrow, "It seems that, no matter what, it is impossible to bring all the necessary causes and conditions together. I won't be able to open this terma gateway in this lifetime. I can only aspire to open it in a future life."

There are precedents in history for a terma gateway not being opened due to the lack of favorable causes and conditions. For example, Padmasambhava prophesied that, if Gungtang Gyalpo

The great Jigme Phuntsok Rinpoche was in great sorrow when, because all the favorable causes and conditions were ruined, he failed to open Mountain Drongri's terma gateway, 1992.

could open a terma gateway at Mount Mo, all living beings of Jambudvipa would enjoy prosperity and happiness for thirteen years. However, due to demonic obstacles, the terma gateway was not opened as wished.

Grand Dharma Assemblies

Every year, Larung Gar Five Sciences Buddhist Academy holds several grand Dharma assemblies: the Vidyadhara assembly in the first month of the Tibetan calendar,[115] the Vajrasattva assembly in the fourth month,[116] the clouds of Samantabhadra offering assembly in the sixth month,[117] and the Pure Land assembly in the ninth month.[118] Jigme Phuntsok Rinpoche organized these Dharma assemblies, in addition to his regular teaching, for practitioners and devotees who were unable to engage in full-time hearing, contemplating, and meditating. Attending the assemblies provided people a great opportunity to accumulate favorable karmic connections with the Dharma.

The first Vidyadhara Dharma assembly held at Larung Gar was a grand event, helping to generate strong faith in the hearts of the monastics and laypeople who came from all over the world. According to statistics, in addition to laypeople, over thirty-eight thousand monastics attended this Dharma assembly. The hillsides were full of monastics adorned in yellow *namjars*, a ceremonial wrap worn on special occasions. Altogether, they shimmered with a dazzling golden light that seemed to outshine even the sun. Ever since then, every year Buddhists from all directions come to the Larung Valley to attend the Vidyadhara Dharma assembly. It is unprecedented to see such a large-scale Buddhist event happening during the degenerate time.

In 1994, Jigme Phuntsok Rinpoche revealed a terma concealed by Padmasambhava on the practice of Vajrasattva. According to Padmasambhava's prophecy, this practice is of immense benefit to sentient beings, especially those living in the Han area of China. Therefore, in addition to propagating this practice in China and overseas, Jigme Phuntsok Rinpoche organized an eight-day Vajra-sattva Dharma assembly every year starting from the eighth day of the Saga Dawa month. A great number of people, monastics and laypeople included, participated in this Dharma assembly each year.

Throughout his life, Jigme Phuntsok Rinpoche attached great importance to *The King of Aspiration Prayers of Samantabhadra*. He provided substantial funds every year to make the corresponding offerings. In particular, he arranged three thousand units of each of the five offerings—butter lamps, pure water, food, incense, and flowers—every day that did not host an assembly. During the eight-day Dharma assembly of the clouds of Samantabhadra offering, he would increase each of the five offerings to one hundred thousand units. On seeing the offerings, such as water, butter lamps, the eight auspicious signs made of flower bouquets, and various tormas made of clarified butter placed neatly in the Dharma halls, people naturally generated faith. Moreover, during this Dharma assembly, the total number of *The King of Aspiration Prayers of Samantabhadra* that participants vowed to recite always exceeded one hundred million. Jigme Phuntsok Rinpoche often said in public, "I don't cling to anything in this world. If I were to leave this world now, the only thing I cling to is the inconceivable merit generated by the offerings and dedications made every day by the sangha."

Jigme Phuntsok Rinpoche organized the annual Dharma assembly of the Pure Land at the Buddhist academy.[119] In addition, he often traveled to other places to host such Dharma assemblies, urging participants to aspire for rebirth in the Blissful Pure Land of Amitabha. Among the Pure Land assemblies, there were three particularly large-scale ones. The first one was held at the Larung Gar Five Sciences Buddhist Academy in 1993. Silver-white tents covered the whole Larung Valley, and the crowd was like an ocean with no shores in sight. The white khatas that attendees threw in the air were like splashing waves. The sound of the attendees chanting was louder than a lion's roar. No words can fully describe the

The first Dharma assembly of the Pure Land held by the great
Jigme Phuntsok Rinpoche, near the entrance of the Larung
Gar Five Sciences Buddhist Academy, 1993.

magnificence of this event. Rough estimates put the number of
participants at around three hundred thousand. Each of the two
Pure Land Dharma assemblies held later in Nyarong and Tawu had
over half a million participants.

Such large-scale Dharma assemblies were not held only in the
Tibetan and Han areas of China. When Jigme Phuntsok Rinpoche
visited abroad, he also organized several big assemblies that enabled
many people to build auspicious connections with the Dharma.

CROSSING THE PACIFIC OCEAN

With his unconditional great compassion and extraordinary aspirations, Jigme Phuntsok Rinpoche skillfully guided fortunate sentient beings from around the world to embark on the ship leaving the dock of samsara, leading them toward the precious land of liberation. In 1993, he received invitations from Buddhist centers in countries across the Pacific Ocean, including the United States and Canada. Each letter expressed the sincere expectation of his visit. Soon after hosting the first Dharma assembly of the Pure Land, Jigme Phuntsok Rinpoche bid a temporary farewell to the Larung Gar sangha and set out with his entourage on a three-month global Dharma tour.

When Jigme Phuntsok Rinpoche and his entourage were crossing the border from Shenzhen to Hong Kong, a customs official stopped them without any courtesy. The official suspected there was something wrong with their passports and ordered, "All of you must undergo a thorough inspection before you can be allowed to pass through customs." He ushered them into a room where they had to wait for further instructions. Normally such a procedure would take up to a few hours. However, Jigme Phuntsok Rinpoche wholeheartedly prayed to Padmasambhava and called on King Gesar and Tsiu Marpo for help. A few minutes later, inexplicably, the customs official agreed to let them pass as if nothing had happened. This challenging situation was miraculously turned around, thanks to the incredible blessings of Jigme Phuntsok Rinpoche and the dharmapalas. They left Shenzhen on time, took a flight from Hong Kong, and arrived in Tokyo, Japan, as planned.

Tokyo is a clean and elegant city, like a piece of crystal on the earth, which brought a pleasant feeling to Jigme Phuntsok

Rinpoche and his entourage. During his short stay in Tokyo, Jigme Phuntsok Rinpoche gave a brief teaching on compassion and wisdom to practitioners of Shingon[120] or Tibetan Vajrayana Buddhism. He engaged in discussions with the attendees about the relationship between Buddhism and science, and he remarked, "Both science and Buddhism are indispensable for humanity. Science and technology can satisfy people's material needs and improve their lives. Buddhism, on the other hand, brings spiritual well-being and dispels people's inner darkness of ignorance. Thus, the value of Buddhism shouldn't be ignored. If one just pursues material satisfaction without paying attention to Buddhist values, one's pursuit will backfire. Nowadays, many people in Asia, be they millionaires or blue-collar workers, need the nectar of Dharma."

Jigme Phuntsok Rinpoche and his entourage traveled onward to the United States. Their first stop was the island of Hawaii, where there are soothing ocean breezes, scenic views, the aroma of sandalwood forests, and captivating peacocks. One day, Jigme Phuntsok Rinpoche was sitting on a lawn, enjoying the beautiful scenery, when over thirty blond-haired, blue-eyed tourists from North America approached him from one direction, and around seventy brown-haired, pale-eyed tourists from South America came to him from another direction. On seeing Jigme Phuntsok Rinpoche's serene and extraordinary demeanor, they put their palms together and sat down respectfully around him. Jigme Phuntsok Rinpoche talked to them with delight: "Today, you blond-haired North Americans and brown-haired South Americans gather here with me, a black-haired Tibetan old man. This is truly an auspicious omen." Then Jigme Phuntsok Rinpoche gave them a brief teaching on the value of life. In the end, this group of over one hundred people took refuge in the Three Jewels.

One afternoon, a volcano near a city in southern Hawaii erupted. The lava caused a fire that quickly spread beyond control. Some local residents were very frightened, so they went to see Jigme Phuntsok Rinpoche for blessings. Jigme Phuntsok Rinpoche told his attendants, "Over a thousand years ago, when Mount Hepori in the Tibetan region was on fire, Nanam Dorjé Dudjom used his supernatural powers to extinguish the fire. Since I am considered the incarnation of Nanam Dorjé Dudjom, though it's only a mere name for me, I hope I can help extinguish the volcanic fire." He then took out his phurba and started to chant mantras. It was not long before a phone call came in saying that the fire was under control.

During his stay in Hawaii, Jigme Phuntsok Rinpoche was also invited to Nechung Dorjé Drayang Ling Monastery, and there he bestowed the Vajrakilaya empowerment on the sangha members and other Buddhist devotees.

AT DHARMA CENTERS IN AMERICA

Jigme Phuntsok Rinpoche visited the United States during the hottest months of July and August, bringing with him the cool breeze of Dharma. After Hawaii, Jigme Phuntsok Rinpoche and his entourage flew to San Francisco, where they took a brief rest before heading to the Vajradhatu Buddhist center in Colorado. Vajradhatu was an umbrella organization founded by Chögyam Trungpa Rinpoche (1940–1987). It was later renamed Shambhala International and would eventually include over one hundred Shambhala meditation centers and retreat centers in North America and Europe. Vajradhatu was one of the biggest Dharma groups in America. Upon arrival at the center in Colorado, Jigme Phuntsok Rinpoche received a heartfelt welcome and reception.

The next day, Jigme Phuntsok Rinpoche went to Karma Dzong Meditation Center. The center organized a grand congregation with many attendees, including great masters, monastics, lay practitioners, and non-Buddhists from several different countries. In the magnificent main hall, Jigme Phuntsok Rinpoche sat on a throne and gave an uplifting teaching on compassion in Buddhism.

A few days later, he went to the Rocky Mountain Dharma Center, where some practitioners had been in retreat for six years. Upon the retreatants' request for pith instructions, Jigme Phuntsok Rinpoche gave them the quintessence of the Dzogchen teachings, including *The Flight of the Garuda* and *The Great Perfection of the Peaceful Manjushri*. Through Jigme Phuntsok Rinpoche's pith instructions, some retreatants recognized the true nature of reality; others gained supreme insights and extraordinary experiences in the Great Perfection, although they hadn't yet completely recognized the nature of reality. The retreatants could not help but

Jigme Phuntsok Rinpoche with members of Dorjé Kasung at the
Vajradhatu Buddhist center, Colorado, United States, 1993.

generate strong appreciation for and trust in Jigme Phuntsok Rinpoche's high level of realization. On one occasion, Jigme Phuntsok
Rinpoche joyfully remarked, "Many Westerners have utmost trust
in Vajrayana teachings and fervent devotion to their lamas, so it is
not difficult at all for them to realize Dzogchen." During his stay
at this center, he also consecrated and blessed a newly constructed
stupa and participated in a lamp lighting ceremony for the celebration of the Fourth of July—America's Independence Day.

Jigme Phuntsok Rinpoche then went to Ati-Ling, a retreat center
of Tibetan Buddhism near Napa Valley in California, and there he
held a Dharma assembly that lasted ten days. He imparted *Chetsün
Nyingtik*[121] and other profound tantric teachings to the attendees.
During this time, Jigme Phuntsok Rinpoche visited a nearby aquarium with his entourage, where he blessed the animals by reciting
the buddhas' names. He remarked, "All these animals are confined,
like staying in prison. How very sad!" At the aquarium, some animals were trained to give entertaining shows to impress visitors.
In one show, a dolphin competed with a man in swimming. With

graceful movements and superior swimming skills, the dolphin sometimes stood upright on the water's surface and at other times dove to the bottom of the pool. The dolphin's performance received roaring cheers from the audience. But Jigme Phuntsok Rinpoche said sadly, "Poor animals! They are constantly trained to become tools for people's entertainment. If we, as humans, are unaware of the law of karma and don't seek liberation from samsara but instead focus only on what to eat and where to find entertainment in life, we are essentially living a life no different from that of an animal."

On the final day of the Dharma assembly, the atmosphere reached its climax. After bestowing the longevity empowerment on the attendees, Jigme Phuntsok Rinpoche led everyone to make a grand tsok offering. Lamas offered precious mandala sets to Jigme Phuntsok Rinpoche as tokens of gratitude from their Dharma centers. Five Western female Buddhists, dressed in the attire of the Five Dakinis[122] and adorned with the five-buddha crowns, performed the vajra dance with khatas of five colors in their hands, praying for Jigme Phuntsok Rinpoche's longevity. Later, Rinpoche visited Rigdzin Ling, where he bestowed the empowerment of *The Practice of Padmasambhava: Dispelling All Obstacles on the Path*.[123]

On the next day, Jigme Phuntsok Rinpoche went to the Tashi Choling Center for Buddhist Studies, located in Oregon. Accompanied by Gyatrul Rinpoche (1925–2023), he consecrated the large outdoor Vajrasattva statue at the center. The statue was incredibly vivid, inspiring a strong sense of veneration among its observers, and the serene and pleasant surroundings added vivacity to the sublime statue. In a Unitarian church in Oregon, Jigme Phuntsok Rinpoche gave a teaching on the *phowa* practice,[124] bestowed the longevity empowerment, and recited the sadhana for long life, as per the requests of the attendees. The next day he returned to San Francisco to lead a refuge ceremony for the public and bestow the empowerment of *The Wisdom Warrior Manjushri* at Yeshe Nyingpo Orgyen Dorjé Den.

The great Jigme Phuntsok Rinpoche bestowing the Vajrakilaya empowerment, Napa Valley, California, United States, 1993.

In Washington, DC, and New York

In late July 1993, amid many people's reluctance to let him go, Jigme Phuntsok Rinpoche and his entourage left the West Coast and flew to the East Coast, arriving in the US capital, Washington, DC. Jigme Phuntsok Rinpoche gave his first teaching in the Lansburgh Theatre—now the Klein Theatre. As he walked on the stage, the audience stood up to welcome him with applause. He was then seated on a throne, from which he looked at everyone with loving-kindness. After the audience sat down and the host delivered a brief opening speech, Jigme Phuntsok Rinpoche started his talk.

This teaching happened to be on the fourth day of the sixth Tibetan month—the date that Buddha Shakyamuni first turned the Wheel of Dharma on the Four Noble Truths. Thus Jigme Phuntsok Rinpoche taught the Four Noble Truths and also introduced the history of Buddhism, describing the similarities and differences among Tibetan Buddhism, Theravada Buddhism, and Chinese Buddhism and showcasing the converging ultimate goals of all Buddhist traditions.

Jigme Phuntsok Rinpoche went to Kunzang Palyul Choling Monastery at the invitation of its abbess Jetsunma Ahkon Lhamo, an American tulku, who was recognized as a reincarnate lama by Penor Rinpoche. Jigme Phuntsok Rinpoche transmitted monastic precepts to the sangha and expounded the merits of upholding the precepts. In the main hall of the monastery, he bestowed *The Neck-Pouch Vajrakilaya* empowerment and conferred the essentials of the Dzogchen teachings. Due to the large number of attendees coming from different states, the main hall was unable to accommodate everyone, so many attendees had to take the empowerment and listen to the teachings via closed-circuit television. After the event, Jigme Phuntsok Rinpoche also consecrated the shrine room and a Tibetan-style stupa at the monastery.

Later, Jigme Phuntsok Rinpoche visited several iconic landmarks, including the White House, the Capitol Building, the Lincoln Memorial, and the National Air and Space Museum. During his visit to the museum, he made a point of seeing the Apollo 2 command module. Jigme Phuntsok Rinpoche stayed at the Vietnam Veterans Memorial for quite a long time, reciting prayers for the soldiers and civilians killed in that war.

One evening during his stay in Washington, DC, Jigme Phuntsok Rinpoche went back to Larung Gar in his illusory dream body. He visited many monastic residences and clearly heard the conversations of the sangha members. He found out that there was a serious epidemic spreading at the academy. The next day, he told his attendants, "I went back to Larung Gar last night in my illusory dream body. Many monastics have contracted a serious illness, so we should recite prayers to bless them." It was later confirmed when he returned to Larung Gar that an epidemic had struck the academy during that time.

In early August 1993, Jigme Phuntsok Rinpoche and his entourage flew to New York City, where he bestowed empowerments and gave Dharma teachings at several Buddhist centers, including the Padmasambhava Buddhist Center,[125] the Grace Gratitude Buddhist Temple, and the Dorjé Ling Buddhist Center. On the invitation of Maurice Frederick Strong, then under-secretary-general of the United Nations (UN), Jigme Phuntsok Rinpoche and his entourage had a tour of the UN headquarters, accompanied by the Bhutanese ambassador to the UN. In the general assembly hall of the UN headquarters, Jigme Phuntsok Rinpoche prayed for world peace. Then he visited the World Trade Center, the majestic skyscrapers with 110 floors. On the top floor, Jigme Phuntsok Rinpoche took in the panoramic view of New York City. With the government's approval, Jigme Phuntsok Rinpoche initiated and established the Larung Gar Sutrayana and Vajrayana Center of New York,[126] which was the first Larung liaison center to be established abroad.

After seven days in New York City, Jigme Phuntsok Rinpoche and his entourage left for Boston. At the Shambhala Meditation Center of Boston, Jigme Phuntsok Rinpoche gave teachings on the origin of Shambhala and other teachings, which were well received by the audience.

Wherever he went and regardless of the audience's background, Jigme Phuntsok Rinpoche could always inspire his listeners with his vast wisdom. Be it profound Dharma teachings, worldly knowledge, or just a joke, Jigme Phuntsok Rinpoche could always bring benefit to the listeners through his skillful means. As Sakya Pandita said, "The king is only respected in his own land, whereas the wise is also venerated in foreign lands."

The great Jigme Phuntsok Rinpoche,
Washington, DC, United States, 1993.

The great Jigme Phuntsok Rinpoche, Nova Scotia, Canada, 1993.

THE TRIP TO CANADA

In the airport of Halifax, Canada, Buddhist devotees happily welcomed the arrival of Jigme Phuntsok Rinpoche and his entourage. From the airport, Jigme Phuntsok Rinpoche went directly to Sharchen Ling[127] and stayed there for a few days. He spent the first day enjoying the sun and panoramic view from a large balcony overlooking the boundless sea and the distant islands and city. Feeling refreshed and delighted, Jigme Phuntsok Rinpoche remarked, "Here, there are the blue sky, the ocean, the mountains, and the forests. The scenery is so charming! Among all the places I have been, this is the most beautiful one!" In the afternoon, Jigme Phuntsok Rinpoche was interviewed by a local Buddhist media outlet. The journalist asked him, "You have traveled a long way from the Land of Snows to the West. What is your main purpose for this trip?"

Jigme Phuntsok Rinpoche answered, "My main purpose is to propagate the Dharma, to benefit sentient beings, and to contribute as much as possible to people's well-being."

The journalist continued, "When encountering adversities, what do you do?"

Without hesitation, Jigme Phuntsok Rinpoche answered, "The only thing I do is pray to my lama and the Three Jewels wholeheartedly. Apart from that, I don't do any particular practice."

During the interview, there were a few people sitting around Jigme Phuntsok Rinpoche. Some stared at him intently, seemingly trying to grasp his extraordinary character through his facial expressions. Some sat quietly, deep in thought, contemplating his words. Some were busy snapping photos, hoping to capture all the great moments. The journalist later shared his impression of

Jigme Phuntsok Rinpoche: "He makes people feel extremely at ease. Although he didn't answer all the questions posed to him, strangely enough, he still made everyone feel genuinely happy and cared for. He doesn't exhibit any manner of haughtiness. Instead, he is remarkably serene and humble, which further highlights his nobility. This spiritual leader of Buddhism has an extraordinary charisma which far surpasses that of some renowned, eloquent political leaders. Only such a great noble one can truly bring peace and happiness to all sentient beings."

The next day, Jigme Phuntsok Rinpoche went to Dalhousie University, where he delivered a public talk on the theme of wisdom and compassion in a lecture hall filled to its thousand-seat capacity by local Buddhist devotees and university faculty, staff, and students.

Afterward, Jigme Phuntsok Rinpoche left Halifax and went by car to Dorjé Denma Ling—one of the largest retreat centers in Canada. There, he bestowed the empowerments of *The Wisdom Warrior Manjushri*, *The Neck-Pouch Vajrakilaya*, *The Wrathful Padmasambhava Dorjé Drolo*, and more on approximately one thousand Buddhists, including the center's sangha members and devotees coming from the United States and Canada. Jigme Phuntsok Rinpoche also summarized the quintessential teachings of Dzogchen in concise and simple language and conveyed the pith instructions to the attendees. His empowerments and teachings were genuinely appreciated by the audience. The large tent where Jigme Phuntsok Rinpoche gave the teaching was fully packed. In accordance with the center's ceremonial protocol, the Dorjé Kasung[128] members demonstrated drills of Shambhala training, and the sangha members sang the Shambhala Anthem as a special Dharma offering to Jigme Phuntsok Rinpoche. In doing so, they created the auspicious conditions for the future triumph of Buddhism over negative forces. The drills vividly resembled the scenes of the Kalachakra troops descending onto earth to subdue tirthikas. While watching this, Jigme Phuntsok Rinpoche smiled in appreciation.

ARRIVAL IN EUROPE

After his successful visit to Canada, Jigme Phuntsok Rinpoche's next destination was Europe. In response to the invitation of Sogyal Rinpoche, the author of *The Tibetan Book of Living and Dying*, Jigme Phuntsok Rinpoche and his entourage flew over the Atlantic Ocean, then passed through Paris and arrived at Rigpa Lerab Ling, located near Montpellier, France.

Lerab Ling was a truly auspicious place, with an inviting atmosphere for Dharma practice. From afar, visitors might notice the many meditation tents dotting the landscape. The practitioners conveyed their inner serenity in their speech and conduct. Their deep appreciation and respect for their lamas, reflecting their strong devotion, was even more precious. Sogyal Rinpoche organized a grand ceremony to welcome Jigme Phuntsok Rinpoche and his entourage.

The next day, Jigme Phuntsok Rinpoche started to bestow empowerments and give teachings. The Lerab Ling sangha members and Buddhist devotees from several countries gathered in a large tent. Looking up at Jigme Phuntsok Rinpoche seated on the throne, each of them expressed reverence through their gaze. They chanted prayers with melodious tunes and captivating voices.

Jigme Phuntsok Rinpoche was in high spirits, and after having bestowed empowerments, he expounded on the eleven vajra topics,[129] primordial purity, spontaneous presence, and other profound Dzogchen teachings. Then he said joyfully, "Seeing how engaged you are in practicing the Dharma, I am very pleased, as this is very rare in the present era. Especially in the developed countries of Western Europe, where there is material affluence, many people easily succumb to laziness and squander their lives away. We have obtained this precious human life through the positive actions of our past lives, and we have the good fortune to have encountered the Dharma in this life. While feeling joyful for this, we should also remember that human life is just a fleeting moment. None of us can be certain how much longer we will live, because there is no guarantee that we will still be alive tomorrow. Therefore, we should practice the Dharma, especially the Dzogchen teachings, even more diligently."

During the seven days there, Jigme Phuntsok Rinpoche tirelessly gave teachings and bestowed empowerments, bringing the bliss of Dharma to each attendee. On occasions, based on his own direct experiences, Jigme Phuntsok Rinpoche would bestow precious Dzogchen pith instructions on the practitioners, who were suitable and receptive vessels for this supreme teaching. As a result, several practitioners attained realization of the Great Perfection. Jigme Phuntsok Rinpoche said, "It is easy to realize Dzogchen, but it is very hard to stabilize and reinforce this state of realization. You need to have unwavering perseverance and determination, as well as unsurpassable faith in your lineage masters."

These practitioners sincerely remarked, "We have heard teachings from many great masters of various lineages and are truly amazed by their wisdom. However, when it comes to transmitting the realization of the wisdom mind, the great Jigme Phuntsok Rinpoche is truly extraordinary!"

When Jigme Phuntsok Rinpoche was about to leave the center, many sangha members pleaded with him to stay. They said, "Western Europe has not only the advanced medical technology to treat your illness, but also a peaceful environment and a high quality of life. Most importantly, people here can freely engage in Buddhist activities without any restrictions. This will greatly benefit your Dharma missions."

Jigme Phuntsok Rinpoche laughed heartily and joked, "Are you telling me to abandon a few thousand of my Larung Gar disciples who are waiting for my return, as well as my motherland—the Tibetan Plateau—and all living beings in the East?"

Jigme Phuntsok Rinpoche left Europe and returned to Asia. In Hong Kong, he bestowed the empowerments and teachings of *The Great Perfection of the Peaceful Manjushri*, *The Practice of Padmasambhava: Dispelling All Obstacles on the Path*, and *The Neck-Pouch Vajrakilaya* at the Palyul Dharma Center and in a thousand-person theater. In Taiwan, he bestowed the empowerments and teachings of *Guru Rinpoche Padmasambhava*, *The Deepest Heart Essence of Vajrakilaya*, *The Wisdom Warrior Manjushri*, *The Great Perfection of the Peaceful Manjushri*, and *The Neck-Pouch Vajrakilaya* at Hsin Tien Palyul Center in Taipei and the Tantrayana Treasury Dharma Center in Taichung.

Everywhere Jigme Phuntsok Rinpoche went, people welcomed him sincerely with utmost respect. After his three-month global Dharma tour, Jigme Phuntsok Rinpoche finally returned to Chengdu via Shenzhen. As his plane landed at Chengdu Shuangliu International Airport, many disciples from various parts of China gathered at the arrival area to welcome him. It was said that it was the largest greeting crowd in the history of the airport.

In summary, no matter which country Jigme Phuntsok Rinpoche visited, he always brought auspiciousness, peace, harmony, and the bliss of Dharma to the people. With his compassionate guidance, Jigme Phuntsok Rinpoche spread the nectar of Dharma, enabling many beings onto the right path.

THE DHARMA SOUND IN
THE KHAM AREA

In 1994, the great Jigme Phuntsok Rinpoche visited the Kham area again. One day, by a lake in the Derge region where Tertön Lerab Lingpa once revealed termas, Jigme Phuntsok Rinpoche was reciting sadhanas to consecrate the lake. Many members of his entourage witnessed dharmapalas appearing on the lake's surface, paying homage and gratitude to Jigme Phuntsok Rinpoche, and then disappearing. Shortly after, a big tree trunk was seen floating on the water. Jigme Phuntsok Rinpoche asked his disciples to take it out of the water and put it on the shore. Jigme Phuntsok Rinpoche then attentively performed the recitation of transference at the tree trunk. His entourage realized that beings from the ephemeral hells were inhabiting that tree trunk.[130]

Afterward, Jigme Phuntsok Rinpoche made a pilgrimage to the birthplace of King Gesar and enjoyed the nearby scenery. He also received local Buddhist devotees who came to pay their respects. He visited the Shri Singha Shedra at Dzogchen Monastery, Gegong Institute, Sershul Monastery, Gemang Monastery, and others, where he bestowed empowerments and teachings. At the Monastery of Jumohor Sangngak Choling where Mipham Rinpoche once stayed, Jigme Phuntsok Rinpoche gave blessings to over ten thousand Buddhist devotees by touching the crowns of their heads, one by one.

On the same day, Jigme Phuntsok Rinpoche met with government officials. The day was fully packed with all kinds of activities. In the late afternoon, when all activities were finished, Jigme Phuntsok Rinpoche said, "Although I have been very busy for the whole day and had no time to take a break, I haven't had any discursive thoughts, even for a split second, from this morning until now. This is entirely due to the blessings of Mipham Rinpoche."

At the Buddhist institute at Sershul where he used to study, Jigme Phuntsok Rinpoche walked around and noticed that the institute had become deserted. The monastics seemed low in spirit, and the overall atmosphere was not conducive to studying and practicing the Dharma. At the site where Thubga Rinpoche used to stay, with tears streaming down his cheeks, Jigme Phuntsok Rinpoche recalled his time with his root lama. He said sadly, "Over thirty years ago, Thubga Rinpoche—the Protector of the three realms—imparted us disciples the profound Sutrayana and Vajrayana teachings. Back then, I was a young man full of vigor and enthusiasm, enjoying the Dharma nectar under the guidance of my lama of great kindness. However, everything is impermanent. Now I am old, and the institute has deteriorated into this. . . ." He continued, "The fact that I can widely propagate the Dharma to Tibetans and Han Chinese monastics and laypeople is owing to the transmission of realization from the wisdom mind of my root lama, Thubga Rinpoche."

At his former dwelling, which had been reduced to a trench out of certain causes and conditions, Jigme Phuntsok Rinpoche offered yogurt to the monastics, asking them to put the yogurt in their hands and eat it. Recalling his days studying at the institute, Jigme Phuntsok Rinpoche told the monastics, "In those days, I followed in the footsteps of the past great lamas and engaged in ascetic practice in pursuit of the Dharma. I sustained myself solely on yogurt. In this modern age of advanced technology, I hope you won't be distracted by external affairs. Instead, you should follow the examples of the past great masters and diligently study, contemplate, and meditate on the Dharma. You should not squander your precious life away!"

Despite facing various obstacles in revealing termas due to his refusal to accept a consort years ago, Jigme Phuntsok Rinpoche could still easily reveal many termas owing to his great aspirations made in past lives, and this capacity had been salient ever since his childhood. In addition to the mind termas that Jigme Phuntsok Rinpoche revealed from his pristine awareness, he also revealed termas concealed within the four great elements. Lake Yutsé in Qinghai Province is a sacred site where many past tertöns revealed termas. Here, the silhouettes of the pine-covered mountains against the clear and peaceful lake form a breathtaking panoramic picture. When Jigme Phuntsok Rinpoche arrived at the lakeside, he gazed intently at the lake and then stepped into the water. As he walked farther into the lake, he leaned forward and stretched his right hand into the water. Before the onlookers on the shore could figure out what was going on, Jigme Phuntsok Rinpoche had already walked back to the shore. Out of curiosity, people gathered around him, and they saw that in Jigme Phuntsok Rinpoche's hand was a terma chest. They were all amazed.

Later, in a quiet place at the summit of the southern mountain at the Larung Gar Five Sciences Buddhist Academy, Jigme Phuntsok Rinpoche opened the terma chest, revealing *The Sadhana for the Practice of Vajrasattva*. In the postscript, Padmasambhava wrote, "This sadhana is of great benefit especially to the Han Chinese practitioners." From then on, this Vajrasattva practice has been widely propagated all over China and the rest of the world, and the number of times that people have vowed to recite the Vajrasattva mantra is countless.

When Jigme Phuntsok Rinpoche was staying in a monastery in Qinghai, one night in a luminous dream, his deity appeared and clearly told him, "There is a precious stone kept in a local household. For ordinary people, this stone is of no great use. But, if it is in your hands, it will become a valuable treasure that gives immeasurable benefit to sentient beings." On the second day, Jigme Phuntsok Rinpoche sent people to search for this stone, which they eventually found. It has since become an auspicious object, foretelling the dependent origination of Jigme Phuntsok Rinpoche's Dharma activities.

In response to the sincere invitations from monasteries of the Kagyu, Geluk, and Nyingma lineages, Jigme Phuntsok Rinpoche disregarded his old age and illness to visit them, traveling across Sichuan, Gansu, and Qinghai Provinces. Everywhere Jigme Phuntsok Rinpoche went, the local monastics and laypeople welcomed him with utmost reverence. They always held a grand procession with many horses leading the way, monastics in full robes with khatas in their hands, and householders in festive apparel dancing and singing. Joyful and festive atmospheres filled every place Jigme Phuntsok Rinpoche visited.

In each monastery, Jigme Phuntsok Rinpoche addressed its problems and offered constructive propositions for improvement. He established Buddhist academies in many places, which allowed monastics to study the Dharma extensively. He also stressed the importance of upholding pure precepts as the foundation of the Dharma. He transmitted essential teachings according to the needs of each sangha. Jigme Phuntsok Rinpoche urged laymen and laywomen to abandon wrongdoings and cultivate positive actions and to develop conviction in the law of cause and effect. He asked each of them to recite the name of Amitabha and to practice the four great causes for incarnating to the Blissful Pure Land of Amitabha. Thus, almost the whole population of Kham, from age seven to eighty, started to recite the sacred name of Buddha Amitabha diligently.

FOOTPRINTS IN SOUTHEAST ASIA

After his global tour in 1993, Jigme Phuntsok Rinpoche accepted invitations from Dharma centers in Singapore and Indonesia, setting out for Southeast Asia in 1995.

The first stop was Singapore. Jigme Phuntsok Rinpoche hosted a grand Vajrasattva Dharma assembly there, which attracted many local attendees and those coming from other countries. After bestowing the four-level empowerment of Vajrasattva, Jigme Phuntsok Rinpoche said, "The reason that we cannot realize the wisdom of the generation stage, the completion stage, and the ultimate Great Perfection is primarily due to the immeasurable negative actions we committed since beginningless time. If we wish to realize the nature of reality and obtain sublime wisdom, we must purify the mountain-like obscurations caused by our wrongdoings. Therefore, the practice of purification is indispensable."

At the Dharma center of People's Buddhism Study Society, Jigme Phuntsok Rinpoche bestowed the ultimate Dzogchen empowerment on the suitable disciples. He also transmitted and taught his own terma, which is the lifelong treasure of his pith instructions—*The Great Perfection of the Peaceful Manjushri: Placing Buddhahood within Reach*—as well as Longchenpa's *The Natural Freedom of Equality*.[131] With succinct and to-the-point instructions, Jigme Phuntsok Rinpoche expounded the quintessence of the Dzogchen teachings.

The disciples in attendance paid close attention to his teachings, so as not to miss anything. Owing to Jigme Phuntsok Rinpoche's inconceivable blessings and the disciples' fervent faith, many attendees attained unprecedented, extraordinary direct experiences and realization. They were filled with heartfelt gratitude and earnestly vowed, "The great, peerless Jigme Phuntsok Rinpoche, our Lama of Wish-Fulfilling Jewel, although you have previously bestowed the Dzogchen teachings in North America and Europe, this time marks the precedent of actual practice of Dzogchen abroad. We will not let down your earnest expectations and will wholeheartedly engage in the practice of this pinnacle teaching that is rare to encounter even in a million eons. This is our way to repay your immense kindness to us." Hearing their sincere words, Jigme Phuntsok Rinpoche was very pleased.

He also gave empowerments and teachings at the Bodhi Association of Singapore, the Kong Meng San Phor Kark See Monastery, and other temples, as well as a large-scale Buddhist organization for lay practitioners.

During his stay in Singapore, Jigme Phuntsok Rinpoche advocated vegetarianism and told his disciples, "In the *Shurangama Sutra* and the *Mahayana Mahaparinirvana Sutra*, Buddha Shakyamuni mentioned multiple times the faults of eating meat. A vegetarian diet, even for a short period, can bring great merits."

The Vesak Day, the fifteenth day of the fourth month in the Chinese calendar, is an important date and a public holiday in Singapore. On that day, Buddhist organizations and Buddhist households across the country light lamps and hang Buddhist flags. Throughout the nation, all kinds of Buddhist activities are held to commemorate Buddha Shakyamuni's birth. On this auspicious occasion, Jigme Phuntsok Rinpoche attended a bathing-the-Buddha ritual,[132] during which he gave a heartfelt speech. When he talked about the Buddha's immense loving-kindness, great compassion, ascetic practice, and other virtues, many listeners were moved to tears and filled with fervent faith and reverence.

Jigme Phuntsok Rinpoche also attended a grand Vesak gala organized by the government of Singapore. At the gala, students from the Amitabha Buddhist School and the Manjushri Elementary School performed a show on Buddhist themes. Jigme Phuntsok Rinpoche joyfully remarked, "It is truly admirable and praiseworthy that the government places such importance on Buddhism. As a result, children are provided with the opportunity to encounter and study the Dharma from a young age, so that they can grow up in compassion and love. How wonderful! If every country could do the same, our next generations would be immersed with love and peace."

Jigme Phuntsok Rinpoche's next stop was the neighboring country of Malaysia. In Malacca, in response to the sincere invitation from a local Karma Kagyu Dharma center, Jigme Phuntsok Rinpoche paid a visit. Buddhist devotees were genuinely happy when they finally met Jigme Phuntsok Rinpoche. Their deep appreciation and devotion were reflected in their facial expressions. During his empowerments and teachings at the center, Jigme Phuntsok Rinpoche said, "Throughout my life, I have always considered wisdom, compassion, and faith to be the three most important qualities in Buddhism. Now it's the age of rapid technological development and rampant proliferation of fanatical sects and pseudo-religions. Without wisdom, it is difficult to discern right from wrong and make correct decisions among complex situations. Without compassion, one is not a true Mahayanist. Without faith, one can never realize the ultimate meaning of the Buddha's teachings. Therefore, in my view, all the Buddha's teachings can be encompassed within wisdom, compassion, and faith. These three qualities complement each other, and none can be lacking. If a person aspires to achieve enlightenment without possessing these three qualities, this person is simply having an unrealistic dream." In addition, Jigme Phuntsok Rinpoche gave profound Dzogchen teachings to some qualified tantric disciples. His teachings deeply inspired the attendees.

On the day of departure from Malaysia, Jigme Phuntsok Rinpoche kindly said to the Buddhist devotees who came to bid their reluctant farewell, "I have already bestowed on you the nectar of Dharma. Even if we don't see each other in the future, as long as you diligently practice the Dharma, it will be enough!" With tears streaming down their cheeks, the devotees waved goodbye to Jigme Phuntsok Rinpoche.

RECEIVING BLESSINGS WHILE SICK

In 1995, due to various outer, inner, and secret causes and conditions, the great Jigme Phuntsok Rinpoche manifested being very sick, which brought a shadow of sadness over the Larung Valley. By late autumn, his condition worsened, and he agreed to go to Chengdu for medical treatment. On the day of his departure, the Larung Gar sangha lined up along the road silently with tears in their eyes, earnestly praying for their peerless lama's swift recovery.

In Chengdu, Jigme Phuntsok Rinpoche was treated by renowned medical experts, but there was no sign of improvement in his condition. His disciples were very concerned because they understood that Jigme Phuntsok Rinpoche had achieved mastery over birth and death, so his manifested sickness had outer, inner, and secret meanings. Knowing that modern medical science would not suffice in curing Jigme Phuntsok Rinpoche, many disciples came to Chengdu and supplicated him to live a long life, praying for his longevity through chanting prayers and releasing lives.[133] Jigme Phuntsok Rinpoche kept silent throughout.

One night, in Jigme Phuntsok Rinpoche's luminous state of awareness, Atisha, Dromtönpa, Mipham Rinpoche, and Lama Lodrö appeared together before him. Atisha remained silent, kindly gazing at Jigme Phuntsok Rinpoche. Dromtönpa said gently, "We have come to visit you because Atisha is deeply concerned about you. Not long from now, on the tenth day of the third Tibetan month, the surging waves in the ocean will calm down. Noble man, do you know what this means?"[134] Having said that, Dromtönpa and Atisha dissolved into the all-pervading Dharmadhatu of luminosity and emptiness.

Mipham Rinpoche, in an extremely wrathful form, sat solemnly and earnestly prayed to Padmasambhava to dispel demons and spirits manifested by discursive thoughts. He then resided in the pure mandala and prayed for Jigme Phuntsok Rinpoche to conquer all adversities, to dispel all obstacles, and to ultimately accomplish his Dharma activities through the practice of extraordinary activities. Afterward, he dissolved into light and departed.

Lama Lodrö said with a smile, "Noble man, you should abide in the view that everything in samsara and nirvana is in the state of the Great Perfection. After arising from your state of meditative concentration, you should practice the bodhichitta of *tonglen*, or "taking and sending." By doing so, all appearances will transform into favorable conditions and the bright sun of happiness will arise in your mind." After imparting more instructions, Lama Lodrö also dissolved into light and disappeared.

During Losar, the Tibetan New Year, of 1996, many eminent masters from various places came to Chengdu to make offerings to Jigme Phuntsok Rinpoche, in earnest supplication for his long life and continuation of turning the Wheel of Dharma. Jigme Phuntsok Rinpoche's own disciples supplicated him even more fervently. But Jigme Phuntsok Rinpoche responded with a solemn expression, "Although I can accept your supplication, I have developed a strong aversion toward this turbid, samsaric world, and I've also had enough of this decaying body of mine. I no longer wish to remain in this world."

One evening in the pure vision of his luminous dream, Jigme Phuntsok Rinpoche arrived at a majestic pure realm, where the Five Dakinis gracefully came forth to welcome him while singing a beautiful song:

> You have tirelessly benefited beings in the mundane world,
> And we, the assembly of the Five Dakinis,
> Come to welcome you, the great honorable one.
> You should joyfully visit this Realm of Great Bliss.

Jigme Phuntsok Rinpoche answered with a song:

> Even though there is no trace of desire in your hearts,
> You still outwardly display the signs of desire.
> Great bliss arises within those who simply think of you.
> I prostrate to you—the supreme honorable ones.

Then the dakinis brought Jigme Phuntsok Rinpoche to a pure realm, where a magnificent throne adorned with precious jewels was placed in the center, but there was no one sitting on it. In that place, Mipham Rinpoche served as the person in charge, Tertön Minling was the chant leader, and Rigdzin Jigme Lingpa appeared as a tantric activity master.[135]

Jigme Phuntsok Rinpoche felt immense joy at the sight of Mipham Rinpoche and approached him, bowing and praying: "My peerless great lama, the emanation of all the buddhas: in the karmic land of Jambudvipa, I have developed a strong disenchantment with the misbehaved living beings of the turbid age, and I also feel great aversion toward my own decaying body, so I don't wish to stay in the samsaric world any longer. I would like to go to the pure realm and engage in the pure activities of a bodhisattva to benefit boundless beings. Please grant me your permission."

Mipham Rinpoche appeared a little displeased and answered, "My heart-son, don't you know that the Dharma is about to vanish? Can you bear to abandon your vajra disciples? Have you forgotten the sufferings of all living beings in samsara? Have you forgotten the vow that you are willing to go to hells to liberate beings, just as the swan likes to stay in a lotus pond? The samsaric world with the rampant five impurities *is* a pure realm. Your physical body *is* an indestructible vajra body. Thus, you shouldn't have such negative, discursive thoughts."

Jigme Phuntsok Rinpoche felt embarrassed and said, "Honorable lama, throughout countless lifetimes, you have compassionately accepted and cared for me. Although I have long cultivated the supreme bodhichitta, I am still clinging to my own benefit. What a shame! Although nirvana and samsara are indivisible from each other, I still desire the peace of nirvana. I am too ashamed! From now on, to fulfill the wishes of all living beings, I shall no longer fear any suffering and am willing to continue liberating all living beings in Jambudvipa."

With a joyful smile, Mipham Rinpoche said, "Excellent! Your great aspiration of remaining in the world to benefit living beings is truly invaluable and commendable. Your youthful vase body[136] in the heart is indivisible from the ultimate and definitive Mipham Gyatso. You will continue to benefit boundless beings with skillful means, and your Dharma activities will be ever more flourishing. The stronger the five degenerations are, the more extraordinary the Dzogchen teachings will be. This throne is prepared for you. When your Dharma activities in the human realm are perfected, you will come here with your entourage, sit on this throne, and turn the Wheel of Dharma. This throne belongs to no one else but you."

Next, Jigme Phuntsok Rinpoche approached Tertön Minling and supplicated:

The manifestation of your pristine and all-pervasive
    awakened mind
Is free from the entanglement of grasping and delusions.
You have realized the unchanging truth on the nature of
    reality—
The honorable omniscient Vajradhara, to you I pray.

And at the feet of Jigme Lingpa, Jigme Phuntsok Rinpoche offered the following prayer:

You are omniscient in all phenomena and compassionate
    towards all beings;
You are the mind emanation of the honorable Longchenpa,
And a great yogi of the luminous and vast space—
Rigdzin Jigme Lingpa, at your feet I pray wholeheartedly.

Then Tertön Minling led the recitation of the following prayer, and Jigme Lingpa chanted along:

NAMO,

Buddha nature is present in every sentient being;
Do cultivate the supreme, vast mind of Bodhichitta.
There is no being here who is unsuitable as a Dharma vessel.
The noble ones endowed with the ten powers,
Always with great compassion and loving-kindness,
Benefit sentient beings and venerate the Three Jewels.
Victorious buddhas and your assemblies,
Please come to this supreme place,
Which is emanated from the mind.
Please bestow the four empowerments upon your followers,
And grant us all the ordinary and extraordinary
    accomplishments.

And they bestowed supreme blessings on Jigme Phuntsok Rinpoche at the same time.

In an instant, all kinds of offerings spontaneously appeared, dakinis started dancing and singing, and all vidyadharas happily enjoyed the tsok offerings. Then the Five Dakinis escorted Jigme Phuntsok Rinpoche back to the human realm. Just at this moment, Jigme Phuntsok Rinpoche woke up from his dream.

After this, Jigme Phuntsok Rinpoche's health improved by the day, and on the tenth day of the third Tibetan month, he had fully recovered. Then he returned to Larung Gar.

Spring had arrived in the Larung Valley. The ice had melted, the grass had turned green, and the sun was shining on everything and everyone. The disciples had long awaited Jigme Phuntsok Rinpoche's return. The sangha members stood along both sides of the road, resembling two long red ribbons flanking the winding mountain trails. They sincerely celebrated their lama's return.

To commemorate this experience, Jigme Phuntsok Rinpoche composed *Song of Victory: The Wonderful Sound of the Celestial*

Drum. Also, in celebration of having dispelled all obstacles and triumphed over demonic forces, he held a festive vajra entertainment ritual with all his delighted disciples, which lasted a few days.

LIFE RELEASE AND SUBJUGATION

To most people, life release—a Buddhist practice of saving animals destined for slaughter or held captive for other ill-intentioned reasons—seems to be a virtuous act with immeasurable merit, but subjugation[137]—the act of subjugating hostile forces, also known as killing out of compassion—seems suspicious and is even regarded as a vicious act of killing. The true act of subjugation is, in fact, the ultimate form of life release. One of Jigme Phuntsok Rinpoche's dreams may help provide some understanding of subjugation:

At dawn of the eighth day of the fourth Tibetan month in 1997, Jigme Phuntsok Rinpoche entered a dream. Unlike the luminous dreams he usually had, this dream was very similar to that of an ordinary person. He was unaware that he was dreaming, but everything appeared exceptionally clear and vivid.

He arrived at an unfamiliar but tranquil place. When he raised his head, he saw his root lama Thubga Rinpoche sitting on a high throne, imparting teachings to thousands of monastics. His appearance was majestic, and his look was the same as forty-two years ago, before he entered parinirvana.

Jigme Phuntsok Rinpoche felt enormous joy, and thought to himself, "During the past few days, the Larung Gar sangha members have been practicing Yamantaka and chanting the subjugation mantra. This might have brought harm to the demons and their habitats. Although we are able to destroy them, we may not have liberated them. This worries me. Now I have this opportunity to see my lama, I should consult him."

With this in mind, Jigme Phuntsok Rinpoche approached the throne. Thubga Rinpoche was delighted to see his heart disciple, and his gaze became even kinder. Jigme Phuntsok Rinpoche told his root lama about his concerns. Thubga Rinpoche answered in a gentle voice, "The Yamantaka practice you've done is exceptionally meritorious and of great benefit to all sentient beings. The practice has enabled a true life release on a large scale. If demons are successfully subjugated, the lifespan of living beings will always be prolonged. Thus, we can say that subjugation is the ultimate form of life release."

Jigme Phuntsok Rinpoche asked, "For a yogi who is truly capable of subjugating demons, the act of subjugation is indeed the ultimate form of life release. However, if one doesn't have the ability to liberate the demons, will one's act of subjugation beget faults?"

Thubga Rinpoche answered, "Regardless of whether or not the demons can be liberated, as long as you recite the subjugation sadhanas and subdue demons through the power of concentration, mantra, mudra, and pure intention, the merits are still inconceivable." Thubga Rinpoche then continued to explain the merits of life release.

Knowing that life release could please his root lama, Jigme Phuntsok Rinpoche was very happy and approached closer to the throne, saying, "Since my return from Singapore two years ago, I have saved and released at least one hundred million lives in the Han area of China." Hearing this, Thubga Rinpoche was overjoyed and put his palms together, praising him, "Good man! Good man! You are really the Wish-Fulfilling Jewel of this turbid time. You are truly the bright sun of the degenerate age." Having said this three times, Thubga Rinpoche bestowed the following instruction in the form of a vajra song:

Profound, serene, unfabricated, luminous, and
    uncompounded—
Having realized this nectar-like nature of reality,
May you obtain the power of liberating boundless sentient
    beings
With skillful means in accord with their capacities.

Afterward, Thubga Rinpoche gave some instructions on how to properly deal with the properties pertaining to the Three Jewels, then clearly said, "In the degenerate age, the subjugation practice is of great importance. If it is done without any selfish purpose or hatred, but with the genuine intention to benefit living beings, just performing the formality of subjugation can also generate immeasurable merit. But, in this current era with the rampant five degenerations, many people doubt and slander this practice. Furthermore, some even engage in the subjugation practice in hatred instead of compassion. That is very wrong."

Thubga Rinpoche gave Jigme Phuntsok Rinpoche a Yamantaka statue and said happily, "The Yamantaka practice you and the sangha performed has brought great benefit to all beings. Thus, let me give you this Yamantaka statue." At this moment, the Yamantaka statue had fire emitting out of its eyes, and it appeared very stately in its wrathful posture.

In the meantime, Thubga Rinpoche asked Jigme Phuntsok Rinpoche to move closer and granted him a blessing by touching their foreheads together. Jigme Phuntsok Rinpoche felt a mixture of joy and sorrow—the same feeling he had when Thubga Rinpoche touched their foreheads together on the day before Thubga Rinpoche entered parinirvana. It was at this point that Jigme Phuntsok Rinpoche woke up from his dream and, checking his watch, found it was exactly five o'clock in the early morning.

That morning, Jigme Phuntsok Rinpoche found a Yamantaka statue in his room that had never been there before. It was a single-figure statue with three faces and six arms, which was different from the *yab-yum*[138] statue with one face and two arms that appeared in his dream, and its color was also different.

Jigme Phuntsok Rinpoche gave the instruction that, in this degenerate age, the act of life release would greatly delight the buddhas, bodhisattvas, and root lamas. He then urged monastery sanghas, members of Buddhist communities, and laypeople at large from all over the world to actively engage in releasing lives. From then on, in response to Jigme Phuntsok Rinpoche's advocacy, Buddhists passionately carried out the act of life release worldwide, yielding satisfying results.

A Trip to South China

To help more beings trapped in the ocean of samsara who were unclear of what to do and what not to do, in 1997, despite his old age and frail health, the great Jigme Phuntsok Rinpoche embarked on a journey to South China, where he made pilgrimages to sacred mountains and sites. With his skillful means, he benefited numerous living beings, leaving his footprints over most of South China.

First, he arrived at Mount Emei, one of the four Buddhist sacred mountains. This sacred site of Bodhisattva Samantabhadra is full of majestic mountain ridges and dense forests, along with Buddhist temples and academies of all sizes. At the mountaintop called the Ten Thousand Buddha Summit, Jigme Phuntsok Rinpoche and his many disciples witnessed the five-colored buddha light—the emanation of Samantabhadra. Enveloped in the glow of that light, Jigme Phuntsok Rinpoche led the recitation of *The King of Aspiration Prayers of Samantabhadra* and imparted supreme teachings to his followers on the spot. He was then invited to give teachings at the temples and Buddhist institutes at Mount Emei. Later, Jigme Phuntsok Rinpoche visited Mount Leshan, where he organized a large-scale act of life release.

Jigme Phuntsok Rinpoche went to Guilin in August, when the city was immersed in the aroma of osmanthus blossoms. Many Buddhist devotees had been busy preparing for his visit and could not contain their excitement. They welcomed him at a mountainside villa close to a lake. Every day, he gave teachings to those who came to pay their respects and request instructions. He tailored each teaching to the individual's own capacity.

He also took the opportunity to explore the scenic mountains and rivers of Guilin. When taking a boat ride on the River Li and enjoying the view of the misty mountain ridges in the distance, Jigme Phuntsok Rinpoche entered a meditative state. After a while, he arose from the state, stared at the splashing water on the river surface, and said with a sense of nostalgia, "It seems that I just remembered one of my former lives. Back then when I was Sudhana, I followed several spiritual masters in this city and received precious teachings from them. In those days, Guilin was called the City of Fragrant Incense." After the boat trip, Jigme Phuntsok Rinpoche told his Guilin disciples, "I've heard the saying 'Guilin's scenery is the most beautiful in the world.' Being here, I agree that Guilin has rightfully earned this remark. Nevertheless, you must not become enchanted by the external beauty."

Jigme Phuntsok Rinpoche's next stop was Nanning, the capital city of Guangxi Zhuang Autonomous Region. Here, after receiving his great teachings, many non-Buddhists took refuge in the Three Jewels and embarked on the path of spiritual practice. Jigme Phuntsok Rinpoche also organized a large-scale event of life release. Many crates of fish were saved from the brink of death and given a second chance to live in the renowned River Yong. Jigme Phuntsok Rinpoche recited prayers to bless the fish, wishing the poor beings of the animal realm be reborn as humans in their future lives, so that they would be able to practice the Dharma and eventually attain liberation. At this moment, *The Sadhana of Receiving the Three Vows* appeared in his wisdom mind. This text, which allows one to receive the three vows at the same time, is unprecedented in the histories of Han Chinese and Tibetan Buddhism. The sadhana was immediately written down. In addition, some turtles, snakes, and other creatures were released during this event, allowing them to return to their natural habitats.

Jigme Phuntsok Rinpoche traveled to Mount Jizu located in Yunnan Province. Many Chinese Buddhists believe it is the sacred mountain that houses the remains of Mahakasyapa—the successor of Buddha Shakyamuni. It is also considered the sacred site of Bodhisattva Maitreya. The monasteries at Mount Jizu, along with

many other temples in Yunnan Province, welcomed Jigme Phuntsok Rinpoche's arrival with grand ceremonies.

At the Golden Summit Temple in Mount Jizu, Jigme Phuntsok Rinpoche gave instructions and clear prophecies in front of
the stupa constructed by Ananda and King Ajatashatru. He said,
"This sacred Mount Jizu is the abode of Bodhisattva Maitreya and
is named the Small Tushita. Although this is the first time I have
visited here in person, I have traveled to this place in my dreams
and have had the honor of meeting Maitreya in person. All of you
here have a strong affinity with Maitreya. Those of you who uphold
pure precepts will become Buddha Maitreya's[139] foremost entourage members. Therefore, you should rejoice and carefully observe
your precepts." Afterward, Jigme Phuntsok Rinpoche went into
a seven-day retreat at the Hua Shou Gate in Mount Jizu, during
which many auspicious signs appeared, and he received the extraordinary blessing from Bodhisattva Maitreya.

After the trip to Mount Jizu, Jigme Phuntsok Rinpoche consec-
utively visited Guangzhou, Shenzhen, Shantou, Fuzhou, and Wen-
zhou, among others. Wherever he went, he accepted many new
disciples, who took refuge in the Three Jewels with him, and also
bestowed empowerments, teachings, and blessings on Buddhist
devotees.

His next stop was Hangzhou in Zhejiang Province. He visited
Lingyin Temple, where, in front of Monk Jigong's stone bed and
the stone wall with the renowned monk's handprint, Jigme Phuntsok Rinpoche joyfully praised: "Monk Jigong can really be considered a great yogi, who benefited numerous living beings with his
acts free of any effort of abandoning and adopting."

While visiting the West Lake, Jigme Phuntsok Rinpoche stood
by the lakeshore adorned with willows and stared at the mirrorlike
surface of the lake. He said, "As the Chinese saying goes, 'There is a
paradise above and Suzhou and Hangzhou below.' Just looking at
the beautiful West Lake, one can sense the beauty of Hangzhou.
It is like a celestial realm here. As early as in the Northern Song

Dynasty, the lake has been a popular spot to release lives. Here, many aquatic creatures have regained freedom. May they be soon liberated from the samsaric ocean of suffering." Then he started chanting prayers to bestow blessings.

In the city of Ningbo, Jigme Phuntsok Rinpoche and his disciples made their aspirations together in front of the stupa of Buddha Shakyamuni's relics at the Temple of King Ashoka.

At Mount Putuo, the sacred site of Bodhisattva Avalokiteshvara, Jigme Phuntsok Rinpoche gave Sutrayana and Vajrayana teachings to the fourfold assemblies of monks, nuns, laymen, and laywomen at several Buddhist monasteries and academies. In front of the newly constructed Avalokiteshvara statue of the South Sea, Jigme Phuntsok Rinpoche gave precious instructions to a few thousand of his followers.

SUPREME TEACHING, DEBATING, AND WRITING

Among all the Dharma activities throughout his life, the great Jigme Phuntsok Rinpoche considered Dharma teaching the most important one. Unless circumstances did not permit, he never stopped teaching.

During his studies at Sershul, he would teach at least seven or eight classes each day. As he was very learned in Sutrayana and Vajrayana teachings of different lineages, during his teachings he would often quote verses from scriptures at will, which made the profound Dharma accessible to all. In the present era, there are other teachers who can also eloquently expound the Buddha's teachings. Nevertheless, there are very few teachers who can impart the teaching based on their own practical experience and realization. Jigme Phuntsok Rinpoche taught the Dharma according to his own direct experience and realization. He was one of the very few lamas on the Tibetan Plateau who could provide in-depth and meticulous explanations of the pith instructions of Dzogchen.

Even when Jigme Phuntsok Rinpoche was in his seventies, he continued to give daily Dharma teachings. The wise would gain extraordinary inspiration after hearing his teaching just once. His charismatic voice was full of blessing power, which also attracted many nonhumans, who sometimes would take up the human form to attend his teachings. One day, from afar, Khenpo Depa and Khenpo Chöpa noticed several horseback riders approaching Jigme Phuntsok Rinpoche and then listening respectfully to his teaching. However, when the two khenpos came closer to Jigme

Phuntsok Rinpoche, they saw him sitting there alone. There was no sign of the horsemen around him.

From a young age, Jigme Phuntsok Rinpoche had been very interested in Buddhist logic and enjoyed debating with others. During his studies at Sershul, he sometimes visited Sershul Monastery of the Geluk lineage and engaged in debates with the senior geshes who had studied debate for their whole lives. His responses during debates were prompt and effortless, which reflected his vast and profound knowledge. The geshes there were in awe of his eloquence, and exclaimed in appreciation, "This young monk, who has rarely set foot in the debate courtyard, possesses such extraordinary debating skills. He is truly remarkable!"

When encountering Buddhists who held conflicting views, Jigme Phuntsok Rinpoche would refute them with convincing scriptural evidence and logical reasoning, which would often leave them speechless. When facing atheists and tirthikas, he would burn their wrong views down to the ground with the blazing flames of his wisdom. On one occasion when Jigme Phuntsok Rinpoche visited Tashi Lhunpo Monastery, he was feeling a bit sick, but after debating with Geshe Tenzin from the monastery, he immediately recovered.

Unlike ordinary people who consult references when writing an article or a book, Jigme Phuntsok Rinpoche never had to rely on references. All his works were composed of words that naturally arose from his profound wisdom either while he was resting in his pristine awareness or after he prayed to his deity. Jigme Phuntsok Rinpoche was often seen composing his works while chatting and joking with others. It was all done in an effortless and spontaneous manner, unlike the effort and strain that ordinary authors experience.

Jigme Phuntsok Rinpoche once said, "All my works were written through the blessings of the lineage masters and deities. However, in this degenerate age, what's lacking is not the Dharma but the Dharma practitioners. That's why I am reluctant to produce Buddhist compositions."

The works written by Jigme Phuntsok Rinpoche are compiled in three volumes, which cover various topics, including the profound pith instructions of Dzogchen, the poems that express his feelings and aspirations, the commentaries on Sutrayana and Vajrayana texts, the vajra songs of realization, and even works related to culture.

Many auspicious signs appeared when Jigme Phuntsok Rinpoche was composing a work on Tibetan astrology titled *Garland of Flowers*, in which he proposed many innovative views unprecedented and undiscovered by astronomers. He also finished an extensive work called *The Great Treatise on the Science of Grammar*, but unfortunately this manuscript was lost during the troubled times in the Land of Snows. In his late years, Jigme Phuntsok Rinpoche composed a work titled *Heart Advice to People for the Twenty-First Century*, in which he explained the principles of karma and rebirth with the support of evidence from modern science. This book was well received among intellectuals.

Although Jigme Phuntsok Rinpoche had long perfected his teaching, debating, writing, and internal realizations, he had always been very meticulous about his conduct so that his actions were in accordance with the principle of cause and effect. Although he was constantly abiding in the luminous state of indivisible purity and equality, he still appeared to engage in diligent Dharma practice. For instance, he had recited the mantras of several deities over 1.1 billion times.

After bestowing an empowerment, the great Jigme Phuntsok Rinpoche took a group photo with his disciples near the Mandala Stupa at the Larung Gar Five Sciences Buddhist Academy, 1998.

THE GREATEST WISH

There is not a single person in this world who does not want to have happiness and be free from suffering. Knowing there is a place with no suffering, only happiness, who wouldn't yearn to go there? It was Jigme Phuntsok Rinpoche's greatest wish to guide countless living beings to be reborn in the Blissful Pure Land of the West—the buddha field of Amitabha. It was also his most important Dharma activity in life. He often said, "My greatest aspiration in this life is to guide all living beings who have established a connection with me, be they friends or foes, to be reborn in the Western Pure Land. Although there are other pure realms such as the Eastern Land of Manifest Joy, the Copper-Colored Mountain of Glory, and so on, there is no other pure realm that is as perfect in virtue and easy to be reborn in as the Western Pure Land. After being reborn there, we can fulfill all our wishes and liberate all living beings effortlessly."

Jigme Phuntsok Rinpoche frequently expounded on the merits of the Pure Land. Not only did he aspire to be reborn there, but he also urged numerous other beings to make the same aspiration.

In 1989, he went to Lhasa to pay homage to Jowo Rinpoche, a large statue of the Buddha housed in the Jokhang Temple in Lhasa that was blessed personally by Buddha Shakyamuni. Recalling the Buddha's great compassion, Jigme Phuntsok Rinpoche couldn't help but shed tears. He prayed earnestly and vowed to do his utmost in propagating the Dharma, benefiting others, liberating boundless beings from samsara, and bringing them to the Pure Land. Jigme Phuntsok Rinpoche rested in a meditative state in which Jowo Rinpoche, emitting rays of radiant light, spoke to him with a smile: "Noble man, from now on, all living beings who have established a connection with you will be reborn in the Pure Land." This is the prophecy that Jigme Phuntsok Rinpoche received from Jowo Rinpoche.

Lama Lodrö and Lama Chenrezik both prophesied that Jigme Phuntsok Rinpoche would widely propagate the practice of the Pure Land in his later years, which would enable countless sentient beings to be reborn there. Based on these prophecies, Jigme Phuntsok Rinpoche started to widely propagate the Pure Land practice and urged people to recite the name of Buddha Amitabha. He encouraged people by saying, "Those who can recite the name of Buddha Amitabha one million times will definitely be reborn in the Pure Land."[140]

Subsequently, Jigme Phuntsok Rinpoche organized several large-scale Dharma assemblies of the Pure Land, which provided opportunities for people to establish an auspicious and favorable connection with Buddha Amitabha. The three largest Dharma assemblies were held in Sertar, Dawu, and Nyarong, with nearly half a million attendees each. Many Buddhists committed to reciting the name of Buddha Amitabha one hundred million times. The magnitude of this accomplishment is not only hard to imagine but would also be hard for an ordinary person to achieve.

Dodrupchen Jigme Trinlé Özer prophesied:

> In the Larung Valley, protected by the tree goddess of
>   Dzichen,
> Nestled between the sacred Mount Damchen and Mont
>   Ngala,
> The emanation of Orgyen Padmasambhava named Jigme,
> Will widely propagate the Sutrayana and Vajrayana
>   teachings like the bright sun,
> To his fourfold assembly of bodhisattvas.
> His Dharma activities of benefiting beings will be well
>   established,

His pure retinue of disciples will spread throughout the ten
  directions,
And all who have a connection with him will incarnate to
  the Blissful Pure Land.

RETURNING TO THE LUMINOUS
DHARMADHATU

The winter of 2003 was the coldest ever at Larung Gar. During the Pure Land Dharma assembly held in the ninth month of the Tibetan calendar, Jigme Phuntsok Rinpoche spoke to his fourfold disciples with a seemingly profound implication, "This might be my last time talking to you in such a way, but I believe we will definitely reunite in the Pure Land in the near future."

In the tenth month of the Tibetan calendar, while teaching *The Mahayana Uttaratantra Shastra* to the sangha, Jigme Phuntsok Rinpoche manifested illness and left Larung Gar for Barkam and Chengdu to seek medical treatment. His disciples were deeply concerned and beseeched their peerless lama to live long in this world.

There are different prophecies from great masters regarding the lifespan of Jigme Phuntsok Rinpoche. Some prophesied he would live until his sixties, some his seventies, and others his eighties. However, Jigme Phuntsok Rinpoche told his disciples, "Originally, I could only live until the age of sixty-seven in this world, but due to your immense virtuous actions of liberating animals and chanting prayers, I could live longer than my destined life expectancy. Other prophecies about my lifespan are only omens carrying certain hidden meanings. I won't be able to live that long."

The prophecies given by noble beings often carry hidden meaning, and there are such instances in history. For example, once a dakini prophesied that Longchenpa would continue living in this world for many more years, but Longchenpa told his disciples, "The dakini's language sometimes counts a year as 365 days and sometimes as one month, so what will happen may not accord with the prophecy's literal meaning." It was true that Longchenpa did not live as long as prophesied and passed away at the age of fifty-five.

In Chengdu, Jigme Phuntsok Rinpoche underwent heart surgery, which seemed to be a great success. His attendants joyfully remarked, "You look great! It seems that you'll soon recover." But Jigme Phuntsok Rinpoche replied, "It may not be the case. Apparently, you are all fooled." In the following days, Jigme Phuntsok Rinpoche talked about the instructions given by ancient great masters right before their parinirvana and their states at the moment of death. These were all subtle revealing signs.

On January 7, 2004, Jigme Phuntsok Rinpoche felt unwell and murmured to himself, "Now it is the recitation time." He started to recite a special tantric text that he had most valued for his entire life. His facial expression turned extremely serene and peaceful. Shortly after, he asked his attendant to help him sit upright. Sitting straight and still, Jigme Phuntsok Rinpoche gazed into the space in front of him and gradually dissolved into the primordial, luminous Dharmadhatu.

The protector of sentient beings, the guide of the three realms, the peerless kind teacher of all, the Dharma King of Wish-Fulfilling Jewel, the great Jigme Phuntsok Rinpoche, entered parinirvana. This occurred on the fifteenth day of the eleventh Tibetan month, the auspicious Day of Buddha Amitabha.

Later, the sacred body of Jigme Phuntsok Rinpoche was brought back to the Larung Gar Five Sciences Buddhist Academy and, seven days later, enshrined in the Vajrasattva Hall for sangha members and devout laypeople to venerate. His sacred body shrank day by day. Jigme Phuntsok Rinpoche had weighed over 220 pounds and was five feet eleven, but after he passed away, people who came to offer veneration couldn't help but exclaim, "The great Jigme Phuntsok Rinpoche's physical body has shrunk so obviously."

Jigme Phuntsok Rinpoche once said, "In this lifetime, I have widely given the Dzogchen teachings, which should have been kept secret. Therefore, my physical body may not shrink after I pass away." But reality proved he was just being humble when saying it.

The sacred body of the great Jigme Phuntsok Rinpoche (on the altar)
has significantly shrunk in size.

While people were venerating his sacred body, Jigme Phuntsok
Rinpoche's head automatically turned to the west several times,
and his face also faced the west. After being moved back to its original position, his head always turned to the west again. This indicated that the Blissful Pure Land of the West is the pure realm that
Jigme Phuntsok Rinpoche took rebirth in. Meanwhile, colorful
rainbows in various shapes, as well as oval and ladder-shaped light
spheres, appeared in the sky. According to the tantras of the Great
Perfection, these signs indicate that the practitioner has attained
the completely perfect enlightenment in this very life.

The grand cremation ceremony was held on the third day of
the twelfth Tibetan month. The funeral pyre was lit at six o'clock
in the morning. After several hours of cremation, the steel bars
on the cremation stupa were all melted down by the flames, but
Jigme Phuntsok Rinpoche's heart remained intact, which is truly
remarkable. Many great enlightened masters, such as Longchenpa
and Jamgön Kongtrul Rinpoche, also left an indestructible vajra
heart after their cremation.

The great Jigme Phuntsok Rinpoche's cremation stupa.

Before his passing, Jigme Phuntsok Rinpoche told his disciples, "You don't need to search for my reincarnated child or construct a memorial stupa for me. I will be with you in another way."

He also said, "Even when I am not in this world anymore, I hope all my disciples will steadfastly practice and propagate the Dharma, striving to pass down the wisdom torch of Dharma from one generation to another. This would be the best way to commemorate me and repay my kindness."

He said, "After my passing, I sincerely hope that you will not lose faith in the Dharma. The Larung Gar Five Sciences Buddhist Academy should continue to exist."

The Larung Gar Five Sciences Buddhist Academy, 2017.

In particular, the final advice that the great Jigme Phuntsok Rinpoche left for his disciples is worth contemplating repeatedly by everyone. It goes:

> Do not lose your own stance.
> Do not disturb others' minds.

For truly enlightened masters, there is freedom beyond life and death, and there is neither arising nor disappearing. Whatever happens in them is just a skillful manifestation for the benefit of sentient beings. Therefore, although the great Jigme Phuntsok Rinpoche's physical body has departed from us, his Dharma body is and will always be with us. As long as we pray to him wholeheartedly at all times, his blessings will always be present.

APPENDIX A

Dzogchen Lineage of Jigme Phuntsok Rinpoche

The chart on the next page illustrates the Dzogchen lineage tree of Jigme Phuntsok Rinpoche.

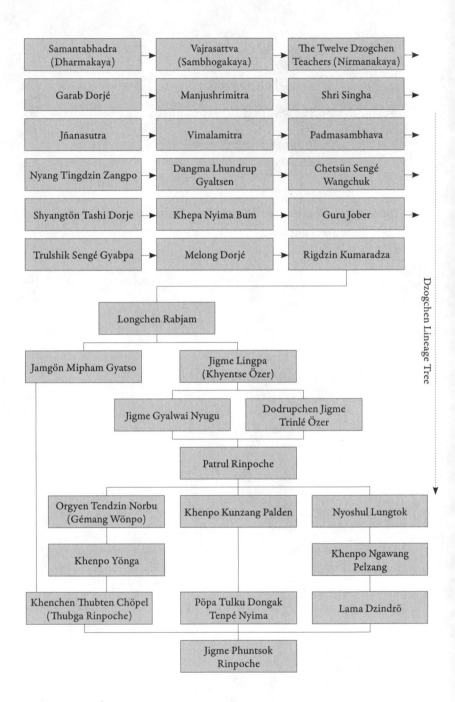

Samantabhadra (Dharmakaya)	→	Vajrasattva (Sambhogakaya)	→	The Twelve Dzogchen Teachers (Nirmanakaya)	→
Garab Dorjé	→	Manjushrimitra	→	Shri Singha	→
Jñanasutra	→	Vimalamitra	→	Padmasambhava	→
Nyang Tingdzin Zangpo	→	Dangma Lhundrup Gyaltsen	→	Chetsün Sengé Wangchuk	→
Shyangtön Tashi Dorje	→	Khepa Nyima Bum	→	Guru Jober	→
Trulshik Sengé Gyabpa	→	Melong Dorjé	→	Rigdzin Kumaradza	→

Longchen Rabjam

Jamgön Mipham Gyatso

Jigme Lingpa (Khyentse Özer)

Jigme Gyalwai Nyugu

Dodrupchen Jigme Trinlé Özer

Patrul Rinpoche

Orgyen Tendzin Norbu (Gémang Wönpo)

Khenpo Kunzang Palden

Nyoshul Lungtok

Khenpo Yönga

Khenpo Ngawang Pelzang

Khenchen Thubten Chöpel (Thubga Rinpoche)

Pöpa Tulku Dongak Tenpé Nyima

Lama Dzindrö

Jigme Phuntsok Rinpoche

Dzogchen Lineage Tree

APPENDIX B

Song of Happiness and Celebration[141]

JIGME PHUNTSOK RINPOCHE

At the magical display of the Five-Peaked Mountains
Surrounded by thousands of bodhisattvas, courageous Manjushri
Illuminated a limitless display of enlightened manifestation.
He shared a boundless, joyful celebration with fortunate ones.

It is said that, just by arriving at this sacred place, all negativity is
purified!
When I heard this truth spoken by the enlightened masters,
It brought a flood of joy and tears to my eyes.
In that moment, goosebumps danced across my body.

Ten thousand devoted Tibetans gathered together.
We made profound and vast practice, offerings, and aspirations.
These are signs and indications that, in the near future,
Our own pure reality will become that of Manjushri and the
enlightened assembly together in one place.

From this moment and in all our future lifetimes,
The father, youthful Manjushri, rests at the crown of our heads as
We tour this illusory city of samsara.
We planted the seed to help all beings, who have each been our
mother.

We found that omniscient Manjushri is our personal deity.
The enlightened teachings are flawless and undistorted ambrosia.

Everything is poured into the vase of perfect memory and
  courageous mind.
We received this sublime, great fortune without hindrance.

Look up: clouds and rainbows elegantly appear,
More beautiful than any painting or design.
Spread across the sky are enlightened images, sacred script, and
  sublime instruments as
The manifestation of youthful Manjushri's dynamic energy.

Look straight ahead: one sees the mountains, villages, trees, and
  flowers are
The natural expression of Manjushri's enlightened qualities and
  characteristics.
It surpasses even the god realm.
We have arrived at this enlightened realm without leaving our
  bodies behind.

Look down: one sees this place and everyone living here.
They relinquish their attachment to this life.
They clearly show their devotion, compassion, and love.
We see them clearly as the audience of Manjushri.

Look inward at your own mind as if it is simply a rainbow.
If you search for it, you can't find it; if you rest, it is clearly
  shining.
This deep relationship with Manjushri has always been part of
  your nature.
Though never seen before, today you see it clearly.

There is no need for heavy effort or burdensome analysis.
In the heart center of this enlightened realm, the fresh, inner
  luminosity aspect of enlightenment,
One's own pristine awareness is Manjushri and his assembly
  gathered together

To celebrate and share magnificent Dharma with all beings.

This enlightened realm, the sublime conduct of the bodhisattvas,
And the vast, profound Dharma satisfies those who are seeking
 liberation.
This experience is hard to even dream of!
Yet we all found this extraordinary experience together.

From now on, even if we are sleepy and lazy,
We have made this connection with Manjushri's enlightened
 realm.
We were sincerely motivated and made so many aspirations.
We gained confidence to go from one happiness to even greater
 happiness.

Living is joyful, as we benefit others and spread the Dharma.
Dying is joyful, as we are definitely going to an enlightened
 realm.

Whatever we do, we are joyful.
This is the kindness and bodhisattva wisdom of Manjushri.

To repay his kindness until the end of the sky,
I will serve the great mission to accomplish the happiness and
 well-being of limitless beings
Wholeheartedly and without ever being discouraged.
Father Manjushri, please grant your blessings, power, and
 strength!

This was written by Ngawang Lodrö Tsungmé (Jigme Phuntsok
Rinpoche) at the Sredmedbu[142] cave at Wutaishan (Mount Wutai,
or Five-Peaked Mountains) as it naturally arose in his mind.[143]

Appendix C

Heartfelt Advice from the Essential Heart[144]

Jigme Phuntsok Rinpoche

Throughout time and space, all buddhas and their heirs are
  united in body, speech, and mind.
This manifests in the perfect example of physical form as
You, youthful Manjushri, the sun of speech.
May our minds turn toward the path to enlightenment.

There are so many different audiences with different capacities.
There is a profound and vast Dharma to be taught accordingly.
All these teachings are brought together and condensed here as a
  practice to apply in one's life.
I want to offer this heartfelt advice to my most heartfelt friends.

If you obsess about only this life, you won't take the opportunity
  to practice Dharma.
The more you indulge in pleasure through the five senses, the
  more you crave it.
This pursuit of discovery, pleasure, fame, and praise is endless.
It's like buying and selling in a dream. Let go of it!

If you have found a spiritual teacher, all good qualities increase.
All faults and weaknesses are reduced.
By studying with such a qualified spiritual teacher
And by making offerings, serving them, and holding the lineage,
  your wishes come true.

Just as you cannot just wish to have a garden floating in the sky
and have it happen,
All the perfect lives of gods, humans, and the enlightened
Would never have the opportunity to exist without morality and
ethics.
Tame your mind with mindfulness and conscientiousness.

From the beginningless beginning, in samsara's blind darkness of
unawareness,
We each wander alone like a crazy person—until now.
From this moment, we pursue the palace of peace and happiness.
We must enjoy listening to teachings, deep and vast like the
ocean.

Just by listening alone, you cannot understand it fully, and
It's hard to build confidence in the teacher and the teachings
this way.
Debating, teaching, writing, and hundreds of other activities
Build the wisdom of contemplation in your heart and mind.

Even if you are in a respected position to teach on various subjects
and topics,
If you don't tame your own mind, you're no more than a parrot.
When death suddenly and forcefully arrives, it is a cause of
regrets.
Any teachings or advice you receive, take it to heart, my heartfelt
friends!

There are so many Dharma teachings available on all of Buddha's
instruction.
Their entire purpose is to tame your mind.
Don't get stuck on the words, but rely on their profound
meaning.
Once again, I simply advise, take this into your heart!

This precious human life is just like an *udumvara* flower.
It is more priceless and meaningful than a million jewels.
Later on, it's extremely difficult to find this opportunity.
Don't waver in accomplishing this greater meaning of your life!

Death could strike like lightening at any time.
No one knows when it might occur.
There's no time to be lazy for months and years.
Right now, this very moment, you must practice Dharma!

Karma and its result are inevitable.
When it ripens, there is no way to intervene.
Right now, you have wide-open opportunity and freedom.
If you fool yourself, who can save you?

Even a minor amount of samsara's unbearable suffering:
If you remember it, you have goosebumps.
When any of the numerous physical and mental torments occur,
What could it be like? You must have this internal dialogue.

To be liberated from this kind of great fear,
You cannot find a stronger or more powerful guide.
Who possesses this omniscience, great love, and capability?
The buddhas, their teachings, and their followers are the
   qualified refuge.

All suffering in this universe comes from the pursuit of one's own
   happiness.
All happiness and positive energy come from the pursuit of
   benefit and service to others.
For that reason, follow the enlightened ones who are the teachers
   of gods and humans.
It is the best choice to develop the mindset to attain perfect
   enlightenment.

One's own awareness is like a crystal.
It is temporarily clouded by obscurations.
It is hard to reflect profound, clear meditation.
You must clean it with the white cloth of the four powers.

Appearance is enlightened form; sound is mantra; awareness is
the nature of reality.
This has always been the view of realization.
At the same time, when you focus your meditation with the
arrow of this view,
You must master what to take in and what to overcome.

Through yoga postures that regulate the winds and channels,
If you can bring the alignment of bliss, nonconceptual
meditation, and clarity,
You master the illusion of the luminous body.
You must take heart to accomplishment meditation.

When the darkness of the five degenerations spread everywhere,
It is hard for the light of the eight *yanas*[145] to illuminate it.
The heart essence of Dzogchen teachings is like the rays of a
million suns,
Brought everywhere by its wonderful three devotions—through
inspirational, passionate, and confident devotion.

Whatever arises in your awareness, remain in natural, relaxed
expansiveness.
Look directly at the mind's own natural condition and abide
there.
When you do so, you recognize your own mind is innately empty
and baseless yet self-illuminating.
You cross the stages of the path in a single stroke, and you reach
completely perfect enlightenment.

Rest your mind and use the three postures and gazes of *thogal*[146]
    practice.
If you look directly at and remain in the sphere of space and
    awareness,
The darkness of distorted samsara disappears into ultimate
    reality.
You reach the pinnacle of the four levels of thogal experience, and
    you achieve rainbow body.

In summary, though these are but common words and
    expressions, it is my heartfelt advice.
It may not please the scholars or poets.
It was written spontaneously as it arose in my mind without any
    editorial review.
This is characteristic of the sublime Nyingma lineage.

This good work for all beings in samsara:
May they gain the kingdom of the four aspects of enlightenment.
May I never separate from youthful Manjushri's courage
Even for an instant.

This was written at Wutaishan (Mount Wutai, or Five-Peaked
Mountains) in China in the solitude of the eastern mountain where
Manjushri taught profound Dharma to ten thousand bodhisattvas.
It arose in the mind of Jigme Phuntsok Rinpoche (Ngawang Lodrö
Tsungmé) and was written in twenty-three minutes.
Written on the third day of the fifth month of the fire rabbit year.[147]

Appendix D

The Sun of Samantabhadra's Realm:
The Quintessence of Oceanic Prayers of Aspiration[148]

Jigme Phuntsok Rinpoche

Your enlightened body was formed through the splendor of
   twofold accumulation beyond measure;
Your enlightened speech, the melody of Brahma, has sixty
   aspects;
And your enlightened mind is perfectly replete with the qualities
   of the ten powers—
Mighty Sage, supreme deity of deities, turn your attention toward
   me, I pray.

Just as you embraced with intense care and compassion
The multitudes tormented by the three types of suffering,[149]
And set your mind on supreme and unsurpassed awakening,
In order to fulfill the twin aims and wishes of yourself and others,
May I too remain untempted by the allure of selfish peace and
   bliss,
And, until all beings, who are as innumerable as space is vast, are
   freed,
Rely on the adornment of altruistic concern and beneficial
   conduct.
In all my lives, as I willingly enter the citadel of conditioned
   existence,
May I be cared for and joyfully accepted by the sole father of all,
That veritable treasury of wisdom, heroic Manjushri,
And may I perfect the oceanic conduct of the bodhisattvas,

As revealed in Samantabhadra's prayer of aspiration.

In future, when nine hundred and ninety-six great guides
Display the attainment of awakening in this very realm,
May I serve them constantly as the best of their attendants,
And gain the power to contribute to their magnificent activity.

May all beings with whom I am connected, through actions good
or bad,
Take birth, as soon as they depart this life, in the Realm of Great
Bliss,
There to receive prophecy from Ablaze with Myriad Tokens of
Light[150]
And fulfill their enormous potential for knowledge, love, and
strength.

May the faultless teachings of Buddha flourish and endure,
And all beings without exception enjoy the splendor of benefit
and happiness.
This, and only this, is my constant aspiration—
Assure me, here and now, that it all will be fulfilled.

May auspiciousness ripen as a treasure of fourfold abundance,[151]
Healing nourishment for all living beings without exception.
And may ills and misfortune be forever entirely unknown,
As the light of virtue and excellence fills the three domains.

Thus, before the throne of the Tathagata, which is adorned by the
bodhi tree, in the central land of the Vajra Seat (i.e., Bodh Gaya),
Ngawang Lodrö Tsungmé made this aspiration and prayed that
the buddhas and their heirs might bless it and bring about its
fulfillment. The recording was subsequently transcribed by the
respectful disciple Sodargye on the tenth day of the ninth month
of the iron horse year of the seventeenth calendrical cycle (October
29, 1990).

Appendix E

A Lovely Bouquet of Flowers:[152]

A Supplication Offering to the Master of Unequaled Kindness,

Wish-Fulfilling Jewel Jigme Phuntsok Jungne,

Human Form of Manjushri

Khenpo Sodargye

NAMO MANJUSHRI KOSHAYA!
The Sun of Speech [Manjushri] dawns upon the lotus garden of
    your enlightened mind,
The Goddess of Speech [Saraswati] delights in the pristine lake of
    your enlightened speech,
The Masters of the Three Lineages are seated upon your crown,
Embodiment of all objects of refuge, O Wish-Fulfilling Jewel,
    know me.

You are the manifest *kaya* of the Victors of the three times.
Your enlightened speech possesses the sixty melodious branches
    that captivate the mind without exception.
Your enlightened mind is astonishingly all-pervasive,
    nonconceptual compassion.
Grant blessings that my three doors may be brought to maturity.

When the blossoming petals of the doctrine's scripture and
    categories of realization began to close,
By the sunlight of Manjushri's three secrets,

You arose from the golden mountains of the Snow Land of Tibet,
To you who once again brought life to the lotus petals of the
doctrine, I supplicate.

Upon the pristine face of the Buddha's doctrine, like a crystal
mirror,
At the time when afflictions of darkness defiled moral discipline,
You polished the three vows with a stainless white scarf.
To you who accomplished the feat of rectifying the Buddha's
doctrine, I supplicate.

Your spiritual instructions mesmerized the fortunate guests to
suddenly arrive.
Your powers of logical reasoning naturally dispelled those with
wrong view.
Your poetic compositions welled forth from the uncontrived
expanse.
To you who upheld the three qualities of a scholar, I supplicate.

Your omniscient scholarship pervaded all knowable things.
Your morality was free from even a subtle downfall.
Your excellent character illuminated your loving care for all
others.
To you who upheld these three sublime qualities, I supplicate.

Through hearing, you brought the entirety of scriptural
reasoning to perfection.
Through reflecting, you internalized all profound meanings
within your mind.
Through meditation, you spontaneously perfected the radiance of
primordial awareness.
To you who upheld these three accomplishments, I supplicate.

From now onward, throughout the crystal *mala* of our many
   lifetimes,
By excellently threading the silken string of pure samaya,
When you are diligently accomplishing the aim of myriad beings,
May we be lovingly cared for to become inseparable with you.

The youthful white lotus of your pure morality
Is undefiled by the stain of downfalls,
And the pollen heart of your *prajna*[153] is clearly manifest.
O Manjushri in human form, may my fortune be equal to yours.

On the sacred holy day of virtue, when the four noble truths were
   first taught,
You arrived in the sacred land of Maha Sina [Five-Peaked
   Mountains in China],
And it was then that the actual Manjushri took his own seat.
Through the interdependency of this supplication prayer,
May your lotus feet be firmly planted among us as long as
   existence endures.

This offering of the pleasing melody of supplication
Was composed in the pure *nirmanakaya*[154] realm of Manjushri,
While witnessing the spiritual guide Lord of Speech,
As a celebratory offering from a fortunate disciple.

Even if the great ocean were filled with offerings of gold,
This would not be enough to equal the value of a single word of
   your profound oral instructions.
How can the kindness you expressed, both worldly and spiritual,
   ever be repaid?
Although your unequaled loving kindness
Could never be repaid with material things,
And since my capacity to respectfully serve you was lacking,
This poetic bouquet is thereby offered with pure faith!

Thus, among the five peaks of China, on the beautiful slopes of the southern peak at the monastery called Do Dangsil, on the holy day when the Tatagatha turned the first Wheel of Dharma, in 1987, I, the bhikkhu Sönam Dargyé respectfully offered this supplication prayer.

NOTES

1. Translators' note: As a gesture of veneration, Tibetan disciples rarely call the guru by their real name. Instead, they use an honorific name. The great Jigme Phuntsok Rinpoche's disciples, including Khenpo Sodargye, normally call him "The Dharma King of Wish-Fulfilling Jewel." For the sake of clarity for readers, the translation team decided to use "Jigme Phuntsok Rinpoche" throughout this book.

2. *Vajradhara*, or *Dorje Chang* in Tibetan, means Vajra Holder.

3. In the context of the Nyingma school of Tibetan Buddhism, the three inner tantras are the Mahayoga tantras, the Anuyoga tantras, and the Atiyoga tantras. In particular, Atiyoga is synonymous with Dzogchen, the Great Perfection.

4. Manjushrimitra is one of the early masters of the Dzogchen lineage. He was a disciple of Garab Dorjé and the main teacher of Shri Singha.

5. The name means Indestructible Subduer of Demons.

6. *Lotsawa* is the Tibetan word for translator.

7. *Vidyadhara*, or *rigdzin* in Tibetan, means "awareness holder."

8. *Tertön* refers to a revealer of spiritual hidden treasures (Tib. *terma*) concealed primarily by Guru Rinpoche Padmasambhava and Yeshe Tsogyal.

9. Termas, or hidden treasures, were originally concealed primarily by Padmasambhava and Yeshe Tsogyal to be discovered by treasure revealers known as tertöns.

10. The Vinaya is the division of the Buddhist canon containing the rules and procedures that govern the Buddhist sangha.

11. Also known as Thubten Chökyi Drakpa and Minyak Kunzang Sonam.

12. The name means Unobscured Awareness Vajra.

13. Dawu is a Tibetan county in northwestern Sichuan Province.

14. Kalachakra, or *Dukyi Khorlo* in Tibetan, means "the cycle of time," or "wheel of time."

15. Dokham refers to the two eastern Tibetan areas of Amdo and Kham.

16. *Tripitaka* means Three Baskets and refers to the three collections into which the Buddha's teachings are divided. They are the Vinaya, Sutra, and Abhidharma.

17. Here, "that" refers to the birth of Lerab Lingpa.

18. The name means Vajra Power without Hindrance.

19. A dakini is a female embodiment of enlightened energy.

20. Nyarong is a Tibetan valley region located in Dokham.

21. Leling refers to Lerab Lingpa.

22. Transmigration refers to the following situation: for most people, when their wandering consciousness enters a mother's womb for rebirth, the trauma of coming into physical existence yet again makes them lose memory of all past lives.

23. Karmamudra, or consort yoga, is a tantric practice that makes use of sexual union with a physical or visualized consort to attain insight into the nature of reality.

24. A sadhana is a ritual text that presents the means to accomplish one or several deities, who in essence are the ultimate state of a buddha.

25. In Dzogchen, the vajra dance refers to a specific practice or ritual that combines movement, visualization, and meditation. It is considered a profound method for practitioners to integrate the understanding of the nature of the mind into their being. The term *vajra* symbolizes indestructibility and the unchanging nature of reality, while in other contexts, it refers to an object employed in tantric rituals in combination with the bell.

26. Hayagriva is the wrathful manifestation of Avalokiteshvara.

27. Vajrakilaya, or *Dorje Phurba* in Tibetan, is a significant Vajrayana deity who embodies the enlightened activity of all the buddhas and whose practice can transmute and transcend obstacles and obscurations.

28. Dharmadhatu, or *Chöying* in Tibetan, means the essence and expanse of phenomena.

29. This place is at the juncture of Amdo and Kham and located in today's Padma county, Qinghai Province, China.

30. The lotus blossom stupa is one of the eight types of stupa in the Tibetan tradition. It symbolizes the birth of the Buddha.

31. Bodhichitta is the compassionate wish to attain buddhahood for the benefit of all sentient beings.

32. Also Jamgön Kongtrül Lodrö Thayé, known as Jamgön Kongtrül the Great.

33. Dodrupchen Monastery is located at Dokhok, near Jigme Phuntsok Rinpoche's birthplace.

34. The term *khenpo* is a degree for higher Buddhist studies given in Tibetan Buddhism.

35. The five principal topics are Vinaya (precepts), Abhidharma (superior knowledge of phenomena), Pramanavartika (the valid cognition), Madhyamika (the Middle Way), and Prajnaparamita (the perfection of wisdom).
36. The quintessence of his teachings is known as the *Vima Nyingtik*, one of the heart-essence teachings of Dzogchen.
37. "Sprinkling nectar on one's tongue" refers to giving the secret empowerment.
38. Yamantaka is a wrathful form of Manjushri.
39. Patrul Rinpoche explained in *The Words of My Perfect Teacher*: "There are three ways to please the teacher and serve him. The best way is known as the offering of practice, and consists of putting whatever he teaches into practice with determination, disregarding all hardship. The middling way is known as service with body and speech, and involves serving him and doing whatever he needs you to do whether physically, verbally or mentally. The lowest way is by material offerings, which means to please your teacher by giving him material goods, food, money, and so forth." Translated by the Padmakara Translation Group (Yale University Press, 2011), page 145.
40. Referring to the specific commentary to the Vinaya code of monastic discipline.
41. Chandrakirti, *Introduction to the Middle Way*, with commentary by Jamgön Mipham, translated by the Padmakara Translation Group (Shambhala, 2012), chapter 2, verse 8.
42. A second-stage bodhisattva has perfected the paramita of discipline, so all the obscurations associated with flaws in discipline are purified. Thus, the second stage is free from the stains of faulty discipline.
43. Shantideva, *The Way of the Bodhisattva*, translated by the Padmakara Translation Group (Shambhala, 2008), chap. 3, v. 14.
44. The eight worldly concerns are hope for happiness and fear of suffering, hope for fame and fear of insignificance, hope for praise and fear of blame, and hope for gain and fear of loss.
45. The five degenerations: degeneration of life span (beings' life expectancy declines), degeneration of afflictions (ignorance, desire, anger, jealousy, pride, and other delusions become stronger), degeneration of sentient beings (it's hard to subdue and help them), degeneration of time (wars and famines proliferate), and degeneration of views (false beliefs become prevalent).
46. The three sets of Buddhist disciplines, or vows: (1) the *pratimoksha* vows,

or the vows of individual liberation, (2) the bodhisattva vows, and (3) the samayas, or the tantric vows.

47. Subjugation is one of the four enlightened activities for the benefit of others. According to Mipham Rinpoche in his *Luminous Essence*, there are various forms of subjugating activity, including summoning, separating, binding, suppressing, averting, killing, and expelling; terrorizing, such as destroying something or driving someone mad; and creating bad omens, lightning, hail, and so on.

48. A daka, literally "hero," is the tantric equivalent of a bodhisattva and the male equivalent of a dakini.

49. "Struggle sessions" were violent gatherings where people accused of being "class enemies" were publicly humiliated, accused, beaten, and tortured.

50. A ritual cake, usually hand molded from butter and roasted barley flour and colored with dyes.

51. Ekajati is an important protectress of the Dzogchen teachings. She is depicted with a single tuft of hair (the literal meaning of her name), a single eye, and a single breast.

52. Here, "you" refers to Padmasambhava.

53. Hungry ghosts are in one of the three lower realms in the Buddhist cycle of existence. They are commonly depicted as having enormous stomachs and tiny mouths, constantly thwarted in their endless search for food.

54. By using the method of extracting essences (Tib. *bcud len*), one can eat only specific substances and elements in extremely small quantities without consuming regular food.

55. "A sacred mount Tsari" refers to Mount Garuda.

56. The Pure Land for short, also known as Sukhavati, is the blissful buddha field of Buddha Amitabha. It is one of the buddha fields of the five families, located in the western direction.

57. "Wutai" means five peaks. Mount Wutai, also called Five-Peaked Mountains, in the Shanxi Province of China is a famous pilgrimage site for venerating Bodhisattva Manjushri.

58. The Practice Series (Tib. *sgrub sde*) is one of the two major parts of the Mahayoga Tantra section. The other one is the Tantra Series (Tib. *rgyud sde*).

59. Khenpo Sodargye compiled stories of tantric practitioners who attained rainbow body in this book.

60. The Vinaya Pitaka, meaning Basket of Discipline, is a Buddhist scripture, one of the three parts that make up the Tripitaka.

61. Those masters had already achieved mastery in tantric practice, making them free from any reliance on conventional morality and discipline. Their behaviors, although unconventional at times, were guided by bodhichitta.

62. The verse is on page 4 of this biography.

63. Jambudvipa is situated to the south of Mount Meru, according to Buddhist cosmology. It is the human world in which we live.

64. The Rimé Movement emerged in the nineteenth century, due in large part to the efforts of two learned and charismatic Tibetan masters: Jamyang Khyentse Wangpo (1820–1892) and Jamgön Kongtrul Lodrö Tayé (1813–1899), who made strenuous efforts to promote nonsectarianism.

65. In this short text of fourteen verses, Lama Tsongkhapa highlighted the three most important aspects of the path to liberation: renunciation, bodhichitta, and nondual wisdom.

66. Sojong is a practice of healing and purification observed by monastics and lay practitioners when they adopt the eight-branched one-day vow on special days.

67. The name means Lion's Roaring.

68. The *geshe* degree is the highest level of training in the Geluk tradition.

69. The mantra is OM VAJRA KILI KILAYA HUM PHAT. As Jigme Phuntsok Rinpoche spoke Golok nomads' dialect, he would pronounce it as OM BANZER GELE GELAYA HUM PHAD.

70. It corresponds to the Tibetan term *tendrel*, or, more fully, *ten ching drelwar jungwa*, meaning the nature of phenomena and how they related to each other. In this chapter, "dependent arising" specifically refers to the concept of "omen:" an accidental "coincidence" as part of the working of the interdependent nature of phenomena.

71. They are earth, fire, water, and air.

72. The auspicious day is Lhabab Duchen in Tibetan, one of the four Buddhist festivals commemorating four events in the life of the Buddha according to Tibetan traditions. Lhabab Duchen occurs on the twenty-second day of the ninth Tibetan month.

73. Kumbum Monastery, or Kumbum Jampa Ling, also called Ta'er Temple, is a Tibetan monastery in Huangzhong county, Xining, Qinghai Province, China. It was founded in 1583, in the historical Tibetan region of Amdo.

74. One of the four sacred Buddhist mountains of China, Mount Emei is considered the worldly abode of Bodhisattva Samantabhadra.

75. A city located in southern Sichuan. It has the Leshan Giant Buddha, a seventy-one-meter-tall stone statue carved out of a cliff face.
76. A "form body" of a buddha, which appears only to bodhisattvas and is adorned with the major signs and minor marks.
77. A mudra is a symbolic hand gesture.
78. Mount Wutai, or "Five-Peaked Mountains," constitutes a cluster of flat-topped peaks, including five primary ones. The middle peak, the largest one, is over 2,800 meters high and hosts a few temples.
79. Jin Chen, "Sanskrit Chants in the Clouds: An Insight into the Larung Gar Five Sciences Buddhist Academy in Sertar," *Sichuan Today*, issue 1 (1999).
80. Located in Shigatse, Tashi Lhunpo Monastery is the traditional monastic seat of the Panchen Lama.
81. This vajra song was translated from Tibetan by Orgyen Chowang Rinpoche.
82. The Threefold Training includes discipline (Skt. *sila*), concentration (Skt. *samadhi*), and wisdom (Skt. *prajna*).
83. Rigden Magagpa (Skt. *Kulika Aniruddha*) was the Twenty-first Kulika King of Shambhala.
84. The name means Protecting All from Fear.
85. A time when people perform righteous actions, called *Krita Yuga* in Sanskrit, meaning "the accomplished age," "the completed age," or "the age of the righteous actions."
86. Penor Rinpoche was the eleventh throne holder of the Palyul lineage of the Nyingma school and the supreme head of the Nyingma lineage from 1993 to 2001.
87. This vajra song was translated from Tibetan by Orgyen Chowang Rinpoche and Maura Ginty.
88. Mahamudra vidyadhara (Tib. *chakchen rigdzin*) is the third of the four vidyadhara levels. At this level, the vidyadhara's body is transformed into the form of a deity, and their mind becomes inseparable from the wisdom mind of the deity.
89. The very first buddha of the present Good Kalpa, during which 1,002 buddhas are to appear. Buddha Shakyamuni is the fourth and present buddha of the Good Kalpa. The fifth one will be Buddha Maitreya.
90. The second buddha of the present Good Kalpa.
91. The third buddha of the present Good Kalpa.
92. The last king of the Tibetan empire, who suppressed Buddhism and persecuted Buddhists in Tibet.

93. The Eight Great Bodhisattvas are the main bodhisattvas in the retinue of Buddha Shakyamuni. They are Manjushri, Avalokiteshvara, Vajrapani, Maitreya, Kshitigarbha, Akashagarbha, Sarvanivaranavishkambhin, and Samantabhadra.

94. Referring to the six paramitas of the bodhisattva, or the six perfections, which are generosity, morality, patience, diligence, concentration, and wisdom.

95. A Tibetan year is identified by three parts. The first two are the animal and the element. The third part is the Rabjung, which is a sixty-year cycle. The first Rabjung began in 1027 C.E., and we are currently in the Seventeenth Rabjung, which began on February 28, 1987.

96. This life-force stone features a naturally manifested image of Hayagriva above, and below there is the self-appearing script of the Vajravarahi mantra.

97. The sadhana is *Bestowing the Splendour of All That Is Desirable: Fire Offering for the "Neck-Pouch Dagger" Cycle.*

98. The silver coins belonged to the immediate predecessor of the honorable Gyalwa Rinpoche.

99. Khenpo Sodargye witnessed the happening at Nechung Monastery. The dharmapala abruptly took possession of a monk, who then acted as the medium of communication.

100. The twelve deeds are significant events or actions in the life of Buddha Shakyamuni. They are (1) descending from the Tushita Heaven; (2) entering his mother's womb; (3) being born in the garden of Lumbini; (4) becoming skilled in various arts; (5) delighting in the company of royal consorts; (6) developing renunciation and becoming ordained; (7) practicing austerities for six years; (8) proceeding to the foot of the bodhi tree; (9) overcoming Mara's hosts; (10) becoming fully enlightened; (11) turning the Wheel of Dharma; and (12) passing into mahaparinirvana.

101. Referring to the death of the Buddha.

102. This prayer is now often chanted by the Larung Gar sangha.

103. The present-day Lilajan River in the state of Bihar, India.

104. The first five disciples of Buddha are Mahanama, Koudanna, Bhaddiya, Vappa, and Asvajita.

105. I.e., neighboring countries.

106. Referring to one of the Eight Manifestations of Guru Rinpoche Padmasambhava in wrathful form riding upon a pregnant tigress.

107. Mind terma (Tib. *gongter*) is a category of hidden treasures that are sealed in the luminosity of a tertön's mind. In the past, Guru Rinpoche

and other great masters sealed certain teachings with their prayers and blessings. Sealing a treasure in the luminosity of the mind through the power of aspirations is a unique feature of these mind treasures.

108. Earth terma (Tib. *sagter*) is a category of hidden treasures that are concealed in mountains, lakes, houses, pillars and so on, to be discovered later by tertöns.

109. The name means The Youthful with Unmatched Wisdom.

110. *Shravakas* are followers of the Common Vehicle who strive to attain the level of an arhat.

111. *Pratyekabuddhas*, meaning "solitary realizers," are followers of the Common Vehicle who attain the level of a pratyekabuddha arhat by themselves, in solitude.

112. Referring to *The Mahayana Uttaratantra Shastra*.

113. Haribhadra is also known as Sengge Zangpo in Tibetan, meaning Righteous Lion. He was an eighth-century Buddhist philosopher.

114. Referring to the great Jigme Phuntsok Rinpoche, who is normally called Dharma King of Wish-Fulfilling Jewel by others.

115. Chotrul Duchen, or the Festival of Miracles, falls within this month.

116. The fourth month is the most important month of the year in Tibetan Buddhism, since the Buddha's birth, enlightenment, and parinirvana all fall within this month. Saga Dawa Duchen, or the Festival of Vaishakha, falls within this month.

117. Chokhor Duchen, or the Festival of Turning the Wheel of Dharma, falls within this month.

118. Lhabab Duchen, or the Festival of the Descent from Heaven, falls within this month.

119. Jigme Phuntsok Rinpoche held the first Dharma assembly of the Pure Land at Larung Gar during the month of Saga Dawa. Now, the annual assembly is always held in the ninth month of the Tibetan calendar.

120. Shingon is one of the major schools of Buddhism in Japan and one of the few remaining Vajrayana lineages in East Asian Buddhism.

121. *Chetsün Nyingtik*, or *The Heart-Essence of Chetsün*, is one of the most important instructions of the Great Perfection, based on a transmission from Vimalamitra. Jamyang Khyentse Rinpoche had a vision of Chetsün Senge Wangchuk that inspired him to write the precious teaching known as *Chetsün Nyingtik*.

122. The Five Dakinis include White Buddha Dakini, Red Padma Dakini, Green Karma Dakini, Blue Vajra Dakini, and Yellow Ratna Dakini.

123. Referring to *Tendrel Nyesel*, a terma revealed by Tertön Lerab Lingpa. It is

a special practice for eliminating obstacles by invoking Padmasambhava, buddhas, bodhisattvas, and deities.

124. The phowa practice, or Transference of Consciousness at the Time of Death, is a simple, powerful practice of ejecting the consciousness from the crown aperture into the Pure Land at the time of death.

125. A Dharma center located at 222 Bowery Street in New York City.

126. This center is now defunct.

127. A local Dharma practitioner's residence at St. Margaret's Bay, Nova Scotia.

128. The Dorjé Kasung is a discipline modeled on the Vajrayana tradition of Dharma protectors and wisdom warriors whose mission is to conquer aggression. Its members are trained in protecting the space in which practitioners are able to hear and practice the teachings. The protection extends to the teacher, the teachings, and the community that practices the teachings.

129. The eleven vajra topics explain the Dzogchen views in the category of pith instructions, one of the three classes into which Manjushrimitra— one of the early masters of the Dzogchen lineage—divided the Dzogchen teachings.

130. In The Words of My Perfect Teacher, Patrul Rinpoche shared a story about a big frog from the ephemeral hells inhabiting a tree trunk. Most members at Jigme Phuntsok Rinpoche's entourage had studied the text, so they naturally figured out that it was beings from the ephemeral hells that were inhabiting this tree trunk that Jigme Phuntsok Rinpoche had found.

131. It is part of Longchenpa's Trilogy of Natural Freedom. The other two texts are The Natural Freedom of the Nature of Mind and The Natural Freedom of Reality.

132. During this ritual, Buddhists pour scented water over statues or images of the baby Buddha, symbolizing spiritual purification.

133. The practice of releasing lives, or freeing captive animals, is considered a favorable cause leading to longevity and health in Buddhism.

134. This meant that Jigme Phuntsok Rinpoche would fully recover.

135. In a tantric activity, such as an empowerment ceremony, this activity master is in charge of bringing sacred objects back and forth between the vajra guru and the mandala of the ritual space.

136. Youthful vase body, meaning a youthful body enclosed within a vase, is a metaphor in the Dzogchen teachings. This signifies the Dharmakaya in which all qualities are present but not visible from the outside. The

body is described as youthful to indicate that these qualities are pure and pristine, untainted by samsara, and immune from birth and death.

137. Subjugation is one of the four enlightened activities, along with pacifying, enriching, and magnetizing.

138. Literally, "father-mother." A yab-yum statue depicts a male deity in union with his female consort, with the female seated on the male's lap. It represents the primordial union of wisdom and compassion.

139. Maitreya is presently a bodhisattva residing in the Tushita heaven and will succeed Buddha Shakyamuni as the next buddha in this world.

140. This refers to reciting the name of Buddha Amitabha in Tibetan. If one recites the name in Chinese, which is much shorter, one will need to recite six million times instead.

141. Translated from Tibetan by Orgyen Chowang Rinpoche and Maura Ginty.

142. I.e., the Narayana Cave.

143. The text was written in 1987.

144. Translated from Tibetan by Orgyen Chowang Rinpoche and Maura Ginty.

145. The Sanskrit term *yana* means vehicle—that which carries practitioners along the spiritual path to the final destination. The full spectrum of spiritual paths in the Nyingma tradition is divided into nine yanas.

146. *Thogal*, meaning direct crossing, is one of the two aspects, along with *trekchö*, of Dzogchen practice.

147. The text was written in 1987.

148. Translated from Tibetan by Adam Pearcey and Sean Price, 2020.

149. I.e., suffering of suffering, suffering of change, and all-pervasive suffering of conditioned existence.

150. An epithet of Amitabha.

151. I.e., abundant Dharma, wealth, enjoyments, and liberation.

152. Translated from Tibetan by the Light of Berotsana Translation Group.

153. Prajna is Sanskrit for "wisdom."

154. Referring to the physical manifestation of enlightenment in time and space.

CREDITS

The English translations of *Heartfelt Advice from the Essential Heart, Song of Happiness and Celebration*, and the Yanglesho vajra song are used with permission of the translators Orgyen Chowang Rinpoche and Maura Ginty. The English translation of the Samye vajra song is used with permission of the translator Orgyen Chowang Rinpoche. The English translation of *A Lovely Bouquet of Flowers* is used with permission of the translators at Light of Berotsana Translation Group. The English translation of *The Sound of Samantabhadra's Realm* is used with permission of the translators Adam Pearcey and Sean Price.

ABOUT THE AUTHOR

Khenpo Sodargye was born in 1962 into a nomadic family in a small valley of a Tibetan region called Kham. He was ordained in 1985 and went on to become a lineage holder of the Great Perfection (Dzogchen) tradition, as well as a preeminent practitioner and scholar at the Larung Gar Five Sciences Buddhist Academy in Sertar. Khenpo Sodargye was Jigme Phuntsok Rinpoche's heart disciple and chief Tibetan-Chinese translator. He has traveled extensively in North America, Europe, Africa, and Asia to offer teachings at Dharma centers and universities. For more information, please visit https://khenposodargye.org.

About the Translators

The Wisdom and Compassion Translation Group, under the guidance of Khenpo Sodargye Rinpoche, is dedicated to translating authentic Buddhist teachings into languages that resonate with individuals from all walks of life. Comprised of Buddhist practitioners and scholars, the translation team is committed to bringing Dharma students teachings that empower them to engage in the systematic study and practice of Tibetan Buddhism.